# Open the Social Sciences

*Report of the*
*Gulbenkian Commission*
*on the Restructuring of the*
*Social Sciences*

1850 - 1945 - compounded status
through differentiation
and distantiation of
3 sciences

1945 - Present - extention of social
science
Area studies
more universities
leading to
blurring of boundaries

# Mestizo Spaces

*Espaces Métisses*

**V. Y. Mudimbe**
EDITOR

**Bogumil Jewsiewicki**
ASSOCIATE EDITOR

# Open the Social Sciences

*Report of the
Gulbenkian Commission
on the Restructuring of the
Social Sciences*

STANFORD UNIVERSITY PRESS

STANFORD, CALIFORNIA 1996

Stanford University Press
Stanford, California

© 1996 by the Board of Trustees of the
Leland Stanford Junior University

Printed in the United States of America

CIP data appear at the end of the book

Stanford University Press publications are
distributed exclusively by Stanford
University Press within the United States,
Canada, Mexico, and Central America;
they are distributed exclusively by
Cambridge University Press throughout
the rest of the world.

# Contents

# Foreword

$\mathrm{T}$he Calouste Gulbenkian Foundation sponsored, in the second half of the 1980's, what became a first, fruitful phase of the project Portugal 2000, generating valuable reflections about the framework for and main issues concerning the possible or probable trajectories of the Portuguese nation at the dawn of the twenty-first century. These thoughts and investigations have been published, in Portuguese, in the series "Portugal – The Next Twenty Years."

As this initiative unfolded, the Foundation further sought to support reflections and endeavors on issues of a global nature and on problems whose consideration and solutions are deemed crucial to the common search by society for a better future. In this context, a survey of the social sciences and the role they perform, in terms both of the relations among the disciplines and of their relationship with the humanities and the natural sciences, seemed appropriate. The great intellectual achievements of the past thirty to forty years leading to the modern study of life and to the science of complexity, the emerging need for "contextualization" of universalisms (which urges an increasing dialogue between cultures), and the growth of university education since the late 1950's all have strongly influenced the practice of social scientists, yet left precious little room for preoccupations of a structural and organizational nature. In the present state of their evolution, should overcoming the existing disciplinary structure not be considered a central dilemma for the social sciences?

The Calouste Gulbenkian Foundation thus welcomed a proposal by Professor Immanuel Wallerstein, Director of the Fernand Braudel Center of Binghamton University, to conduct a distinguished international group of scholars–six from the social sciences, two from the natural sciences, and two from the humanities–in a reflection on the present social sciences and their future. Consequently, the Gulbenkian Commission on the Restructuring of the Social Sciences was created in July 1993, with Professor Wallerstein as its chair. Its composition reflects both the depth and the wide perspective that was necessary to achieve the analysis presented in the text that follows.

*Open the Social Sciences* is a serious, generous, and provocative book, which faithfully depicts the atmosphere and the vivacity of the Gulbenkian Commission's exchanges during the two-year period that followed its creation. Three plenary meetings were held: the first at the Foundation's headquarters in Lisbon in June 1994, the second at the Maison des Sciences de l'Homme in Paris in January 1995, and the third at the Fernand Braudel Center in Binghamton in April 1995. Its intellectual level is primarily due to the capacity of the eminent individuals who served on the Commission, but the overall achievement would not have been possible without the enthusiasm, determination, and leadership of Immanuel Wallerstein, which we gratefully acknowledge here.

*Calouste Gulbenkian Foundation*

# Members of the Commission

**Immanuel Wallerstein**, chair of the Commission, sociology, U.S.A. Director of the Fernand Braudel Center for the Study of Economies, Historical Systems, and Civilizations, and Distinguished Professor of Sociology, Binghamton University; President, International Sociological Association; author, *The Modern World-System* (3 vols.); *Unthinking Social Science.*

**Calestous Juma**, science and technology studies, Kenya. Executive Secretary, U.N. Convention on Biodiversity, Geneva; former Executive Director, African Centre for Technology Studies, Nairobi; co-author, *Long-Run Economics: An Evolutionary Approach to Economic Growth.*

**Evelyn Fox Keller**, physics, U.S.A. Professor of the History and Philosophy of Science, Massachusetts Institute of Technology; MacArthur Fellow, 1992–1997; author, *Reflections on Gender and Science.*

**Jürgen Kocka**, history, Germany. Professor of the History of the Industrial World, Freie Universität, Berlin; permanent Fellow, Wissenschaftskolleg zu Berlin; Director, Center for Contemporary History, Potsdam; author, *Arbeitverhältnisse und Arbeiterexistenzen*; editor, *Bourgeois Society in Nineteenth-Century Europe*.

**Dominique Lecourt**, philosophy, France. Professor of the Philosophy and History of Science, Université de Paris–Denis Diderot; author, *A quoi donc sert la philosophie? Des sciences de la nature aux sciences politiques*; *Prométhée, Faust, Frankenstein: Fondements imaginaires de l'éthique*.

**V. Y. Mudimbe**, Romance languages, Zaire. William R. Kenan, Jr., Professor at Stanford University, where he teaches in the Department of Comparative Literature, French and Italian, and Classics, and in the African Studies and Modern Thought and Literature programs; General Secretary, Society for African Philosophy in North America; author, *The Invention of Africa*; co-editor, *Africa and the Disciplines*.

**Kinhide Mushakoji**, political science, Japan. Professor, Faculty of International Studies, Meiji Gakuin University; former President, International Political Science Association; former Vice-Rector for Programme, United Nations University; President, Japanese Council for International Affairs; author, *Global Issues and Interparadigmatic Dialogue—Essays on Multipolar Politics*.

**Ilya Prigogine**, Vicomte, chemistry, Belgium. Nobel Prize for Chemistry, 1977; Director, Instituts Internationaux de Physique et de Chimie, fondé par E. Solvay; Director, Ilya Prigogine Center for Studies in Statistical Mechanics and Complex Systems, University of Texas at Austin; co-author, *La nouvelle alliance*; *Exploring Complexity*; *Entre le temps et l'éternité*.

**Peter J. Taylor**, geography, UK. Professor of Geography, Loughborough University; editor, *Political Geography*; co-editor, *Review of International Political Economy*; author, *Political Geography: World-Economy, Nation-State and Locality*.

**Michel-Rolph Trouillot**, anthropology, Haiti. Krieger-Eisenhower Distinguished Professor of Anthropology, and Director, Institute for Global Studies in Culture, Power and History, The Johns Hopkins University; former Chair, Advisory Council, Wenner-Gren Foundation for Anthropological Research; author, *Silencing the Past: Power and the Production of History*; *Peasants and Capital: Dominica in the World Economy*.

# Open the Social Sciences

*Report of the
Gulbenkian Commission
on the Restructuring of the
Social Sciences*

# 1. The Historical Construction of the Social Sciences, from the Eighteenth Century to 1945

> Think of life as an immense problem, an equation, or
> rather a family of equations, partially dependent on each
> other, partially independent . . . it being understood that
> these equations are very complex, that they are full of
> surprises, and that we are often unable to discover
> their "roots."
>
> —Fernand Braudel[1]

The idea that we can reflect intelligently on the nature of humans, their relations to each other and to spiritual forces, and the social structures that they have created and within which they live is at least as old as recorded history. The received religious texts discuss these matters, as do the texts we call philosophical. And there is the oral wisdom that has been passed on through the ages, and often put into written form at one point or another. No doubt, much of this wisdom was the result of culling inductively from the fullness of experienced human life in one or another part of the world over a long period of time, even if the results were presented in the form of revelation or rational deduction from some inherent eternal truths.

What we today call social science is heir to this wisdom. It is, however, a distant heir, and perhaps often an ungrateful and

1. Fernand Braudel, preface to Charles Morazé, *Les bourgeois conquérants* (Paris: Libraire Armand Colin, 1957).

unacknowledging heir, for social science consciously defined itself as the search for truths that went beyond such received or
deduced wisdom. Social science is an enterprise of the modern
world. Its roots lie in the attempt, full-blown since the sixteenth
century, and part and parcel of the construction of our modern
world, to develop systematic, secular knowledge about reality
that is somehow validated empirically. This took the name of *sci-
entia*, which simply meant knowledge. Of course, philosophy,
etymologically, also means knowledge, or more precisely the
love of knowledge.

The so-called classical view of science, predominant for several centuries now, was built on two premises. One was the Newtonian model, in which there exists a symmetry between past
and future. This was a quasi-theological vision: like God, we can
attain certitudes, and therefore do not need to distinguish between past and future, since everything coexists in an eternal
present. The second premise was Cartesian dualism, the assumption that there is a fundamental distinction between nature
and humans, between matter and mind, between the physical
world and the social/spiritual world. When Thomas Hooke drew
up the statutes of the Royal Society in 1663, he inscribed as its
objective "to improve the knowledge of naturall things, and all
useful Arts, Manufactures, Mechanick practises, Engynes and
Inventions by Experiments," adding the phrase "not medling
with Divinity, Metaphysics, Moralls, Politicks, Grammar, Rhet-
oricks, or Logick."[2] These statutes incarnated already the divi-

2. Cited in Sir Henry Lyons, *The Royal Society, 1660–1940* (New York:
Greenwood Press, 1968), p. 41.

sion of the ways of knowing into what C. P. Snow would later call the "two cultures."

Science came to be defined as the search for universal laws of nature that remained true over all of time and space. Alexandre Koyré, tracing the transformation of European conceptions of space from the fifteenth to the eighteenth century, noted:

> The infinite Universe of the New Cosmology, infinite in Duration as well as in Extension, in which eternal matter in accordance with eternal and necessary laws moves endlessly and aimlessly in eternal space, inherited all the ontological attributes of Divinity. Yet only those–all the others the departed God took away with Him.[3]

The other attributes of the departed God were, of course, the moral values of a Christian world, such as love, humility, charity. Koyré does not here remark on the values that came in their place, but we know that the departed God did not quite leave a moral vacuum behind. If the skies were lifted beyond limit, so too were human ambitions. Progress became the operative word–now endowed with the newly acquired sense of infinitude and reinforced by the material achievements of technology.

The "world" of which Koyré speaks is not the terrestrial globe, but the cosmos. Indeed, one might argue that, over the same period, the perception of terrestrial space in the Western world was undergoing a transformation in the reverse direction, toward finitude. For most people, it was only with the voyages of discovery traversing the globe that the earth closed in onto its spherical form. To be sure, the circumference of this sphere was far greater than the one Columbus had imagined, but it was

3. Alexandre Koyré, *From the Closed World to the Infinite Universe* (Baltimore: Johns Hopkins University Press, 1957), p. 276.

nonetheless finite. Furthermore, with use, and over time, these same voyages of discovery established the commercial routes, and the consequent enlarged divisions of labor, that would steadily shrink social and temporal distances.

However, this finitude of the earth was not, at least not until recently, a source of discouragement. While the ideal and the vision of unlimited progress drew sustenance from the infinities of time and space, the practical realization of progress in human affairs through technological advance depended on the know-ability and explorability of the world, on a confidence in its finitude in certain key dimensions (especially its epistemology and geography). Indeed, it was generally supposed that achieving progress required that we rid ourselves completely of all inhibitions and restraint in our role as discoverers seeking to uncover the inner secrets and to tap the resources of a world within reach. Up until the twentieth century, it seems that the finitude of the earthly sphere served primarily to facilitate the explorations and exploitation demanded by progress, and to make practical and realizable Western aspirations to dominion. In the twentieth century, as terrestrial distances began to shrink to a level that seemed to be constraining, the limitations of the earth could even be invoked as added incentive for the ever more upward and outward explorations needed to enlarge that sphere of dominance still further. In short, the abode of our present and past habitation came to look less like a home base and more like a launching pad, the place from which we, as men (and a few women) of science, could soar into space, establishing a position of mastery over an ever more cosmic unity.

Progress and discovery may be the key words here, but other

terms–science, unity, simplicity, mastery, and even "the universe"–are needed to complete the lexicon. Natural science, as
it was constructed in the seventeenth and eighteenth centuries,
derived primarily from the study of celestial mechanics. At first,
those who attempted to establish the legitimacy and priority of
the scientific search for the laws of nature made little distinction
between science and philosophy. To the extent that they distinguished the two domains, they thought of them as allies in the
search for secular truth. But as experimental, empirical work became ever more central to the vision of science, philosophy began to seem to natural scientists more and more a mere substitute for theology, equally guilty of *a priori* assertions of truth
that were untestable. By the beginning of the nineteenth century, the division of knowledge into two domains had lost the
sense of their being "separate but equal" spheres and took on
the flavor of a hierarchy, at least in the eyes of natural scientists–
knowledge that was certain (science) versus knowledge that was
imagined, even imaginary (what was not science). Finally, in the
beginning of the nineteenth century, the triumph of science was
ensconced linguistically. The term "science" without a specify-
ing adjective came to be equated primarily (often exclusively)
with natural science.[4] This fact marked the culmination of the
attempt of natural science to acquire for itself a socio-intellec-
tual legitimacy that was totally separate from, indeed even in opposition to, another form of knowledge called philosophy.

4. This is clear in English and in the Romance languages. It is less
clear in German, where the term *Wissenschaft* continues to be used as a
general term for systematic knowledge and where what in English are
called the "humanities" are called *Geisteswissenschaften*, which trans-
lates literally as knowledge of spiritual or mental matters.

Science, that is, natural science, was more clearly defined than its alternative, for which the world has never even agreed upon a single name. Sometimes called the arts, sometimes the humanities, sometimes letters or *belles-lettres*, sometimes philosophy, sometimes even just "culture," or in German *Geisteswissenschaften*, the alternative to "science" has had a variable face and emphasis, a lack of internal cohesiveness, which did not help its practitioners plead their cause with the authorities, especially given their seeming inability to offer "practical" results. For it had begun to be clear that the epistemological struggle over what was legitimate knowledge was no longer a struggle over who would control knowledge about nature (the natural scientists had clearly won exclusive rights to this domain by the eighteenth century) but about who would control knowledge about the human world.

The need of the modern state for more exact knowledge on which to base its decisions had led to the emergence of new categories of knowledge already in the eighteenth century, but these categories still had uncertain definitions and frontiers. Social philosophers began to speak of "social physics," and European thinkers began to recognize the existence of multiple kinds of social systems in the world ("how can one be a Persian?"), whose variety needed explanation. It was in this context that the university (which had been in many ways a moribund institution since the sixteenth century, the result of having previously been linked too closely with the Church) was revived in the late eighteenth and early nineteenth centuries as the principal institutional locus for the creation of knowledge.

The university was revived and transformed. The faculty of

theology became minor, sometimes disappearing completely or being replaced by a mere department of religious studies within the faculty of philosophy. The faculty of medicine conserved its role as the center of training in a specific professional domain, now entirely defined as applied scientific knowledge. It was primarily within the faculty of philosophy (and to a far lesser degree within the faculty of law) that the modern structures of knowledge were to be built. It was into this faculty (which remained structurally unified in many universities, but was subdivided in others) that the practitioners of both the arts and the natural sciences would enter and build their multiple autonomous disciplinary structures.

The intellectual history of the nineteenth century is marked above all by this disciplinarization and professionalization of knowledge, that is to say, by the creation of permanent institutional structures designed both to produce new knowledge and to reproduce the producers of knowledge. The creation of multiple disciplines was premised on the belief that systematic research required skilled concentration on the multiple separate arenas of reality, which was partitioned rationally into distinct groupings of knowledge. Such a rational division promised to be effective, that is, intellectually productive. The natural sciences had not awaited the revival of the university to establish some kind of autonomous institutional life. They had been able to act earlier because they could lay claim to social and political support on the basis of their promise to produce practical results that were immediately useful. The rise of royal academies in the seventeenth and eighteenth centuries and the creation of the *grandes écoles* by Napoleon reflected the willingness of the rulers to promote the natural sciences. The natural scientists perhaps did not need the universities to pursue their work.

It was rather those who were not natural scientists–historians, classicists, scholars of national literatures–who did most to revive the universities in the course of the nineteenth century, using it as a mechanism to obtain state support for their scholarly work. They pulled the natural scientists into the burgeoning university structures, thereby profiting from the positive profile of the natural scientists. The result, however, was that from then on the universities became the primary site of the continuing tension between the arts (humanities) and the sciences, which were now being defined as quite different, and for some antagonistic, ways of knowing.

In many countries, certainly in Great Britain and France, it was the cultural upheaval brought about by the French Revolution that forced a certain clarification of the debate. The pressure for political and social transformation had gained an urgency and a legitimacy that could not easily be contained any longer simply by proclaiming theories about a supposedly natural order of social life. Instead, many argued that the solution lay rather in organizing and rationalizing the social change that now seemed to be inevitable in a world in which the sovereignty of the "people" was fast becoming the norm, no doubt hoping thereby to limit its extent. But if one were to organize and rationalize social change, one had first of all to study it and understand the rules which governed it. There was not only space for, but a deep social need for, what we have come to call social science. Furthermore, it seemed to follow that if one were to try to organize a new social order on a stable base, the more exact (or "positive") the science, perhaps the better. With this in view, many of those who began to lay the bases of modern social science in the first half of the nineteenth century, most notably in Great Britain and France, turned to Newtonian physics as a model to emulate.

Others, more concerned with reknitting the social unity of the states which had undergone or were threatened by social disruption, looked to the elaboration of national historical accounts to underpin the new or potential sovereignties, accounts that were, however, now less accounts of princes than of "peoples." The reformulation of "history" as *geschichte*–what happened, what *really* happened–was thought to give it impeccable credentials. History would cease to be a hagiography justifying monarchs and become the true story of the past, explaining the present, offering the basis of wise choice for the future. This kind of history (based on empirical archival research) joined social science and natural science in rejecting "speculation" and "deduction" (practices which were said to be mere "philosophy"). But precisely because this kind of history was deeply concerned with the stories of peoples, each empirically different from the other, it looked with suspicion, even hostility, upon the attempts of the exponents of the new "social science" to generalize, that is, to establish universal laws of society.

In the course of the nineteenth century, the various disciplines spread out like a fan, covering a range of epistemological positions. At one end lay, first, mathematics (a nonempirical activity) and next to it the experimental natural sciences (themselves in a sort of descending order of determinism–physics, chemistry, biology). At the other end lay the humanities (or arts and letters), starting with philosophy (the pendant of mathematics, as a nonempirical activity) and next to it the study of formal artistic practices (literatures, painting and sculpture, musicology), often coming close in their practice to being history, a history of the arts. And in between the humanities and the natural sciences, thus defined, lay the study of social realities, with history (idiographic) closer to, often part of, faculties of arts and letters, and "social science" (nomothetic) closer to the natural sciences. Amidst an ever-hardening separation of knowledge into two different spheres, each with a different epistemological emphasis, the students of social realities found themselves caught in the middle, and deeply divided on these epistemological issues.

All this, however, was occurring in a context in which (Newtonian) science had triumphed over (speculative) philosophy and had therefore come to incarnate social prestige in the world of knowledge. This split between science and philosophy had been proclaimed as a divorce by Auguste Comte, although in reality it represented primarily the rejection of Aristotelian metaphysics and not of philosophical concerns per se. Nonetheless, the issues posed seemed to be real: is the world governed by deterministic laws? or is there a place, a role for (human) inventiveness and imagination? The intellectual issues were, furthermore, overlain with their putative political implications. Politically, the concept of deterministic laws seemed more useful for attempts at technocratic control of potentially anarchic movements for change. And politically, the defense of the particular, the nondetermined, the imaginative seemed more useful not only for those who were resisting technocratic change in the

name of conserving existing institutions and traditions but also
for those who were struggling for more spontaneous, more radical possibilities of intruding human agency into the sociopoliti-
cal arena. In this debate, which was continuous but unbalanced,
the outcome in the world of knowledge was that science
(physics) was everywhere placed on a pedestal and in many
countries philosophy was relegated to an ever smaller corner of
the university system. One response of some philosophers was
eventually to redefine their activities in ways more consonant
with the scientific ethos (the analytic philosophy of the Vienna
positivists).

Science was proclaimed to be the discovery of objective reality, using a method that enabled us to go *outside* the mind,
whereas philosophers were said merely to cogitate and write
about their cogitations. This view of science and philosophy was
asserted quite clearly by Comte and John Stuart Mill in the first
half of the nineteenth century as they undertook to lay down the
rules that would govern analyses of the social world. In reviving
the term "social physics," Comte made clear his political concerns. He wished to save the West from the "systematic corrup-
tion" which had become "erected into an indispensable tool of
governing" because of the "intellectual anarchy" that had been
manifest since the French Revolution. In his view, the party of
order was basing itself on outmoded doctrines (Catholic and feu-
dal), while the party of movement was basing itself on purely
negative and destructive theses drawn from Protestantism. For
Comte, social physics would permit the reconciliation of order
and progress by turning over the solution of social questions
to "a small number of elite intelligences" with the appropriate

education. In this way, the Revolution would be "terminated" by the installation of a new spiritual power. The technocratic basis and the social function of the new social physics was thus clear. In this new structure of knowledge, philosophers would become, in a celebrated formula, the "specialists of generalities." What this meant was that they would apply the logic of celestial mechanics (brought to perfection in Pierre-Simon Laplace's version of the Newtonian prototype) to the social world. Positive science was intended to represent total liberation from theology and metaphysics and all other modes of "explaining" reality. "Our researches, then, in every branch of knowledge, if they are to be positive, must be confined to the study of real facts without seeking to know their first causes or final purpose."[5]

Comte's English counterpart and correspondent, John Stuart Mill, spoke not of positive science but of exact science, but the model of celestial mechanics remained the same: "[the science of human nature] falls far short of the standards of exactness now realized in Astronomy; but there is no reason that it should not be as much a science as Tidology is, or as Astronomy was when its calculations had only mastered the main phenomena, but not the perturbations."[6]

Although the underpinnings of the divisions within the social sciences were clearly crystallizing in the first half of the nineteenth century, it was only in the period 1850-1914 that the intellectual diversification reflected in the disciplinary structures

---

5. Auguste Comte, *A Discourse on the Positive Spirit* (London: William Reeves, 1903), p. 21.

6. John Stuart Mill, *A System of Logic Ratiocinative and Inductive*, vol. 8 of *Collected Works of John Stuart Mill* (Toronto: University of Toronto Press, 1974), bk. 6, chap. 3, para. 2, p. 846.

of the social sciences was formally recognized in the principal universities in the forms that we know them today. To be sure, in the period between 1500 and 1850 there had already existed a literature concerning many of the central questions treated in what we today call social science—the functioning of political institutions, the macroeconomic policies of the states, the rules governing interstate relations, the description of non-European social systems. Today we still read Niccolo Machiavelli and Jean Bodin, William Petty and Hugo Grotius, the French Physiocrats and the Scottish Enlightenment, as well as the authors of the first half of the nineteenth century, from Thomas Malthus and David Ricardo to François Guizot and Alexis de Tocqueville to Johann Herder and Johann Fichte. We even have in this period early discussions of social deviance, as in Cesare Beccaria. But all this was not yet quite what we have come to mean today by social science, and none of these scholars yet thought of himself as operating within the framework of what later were considered the separate disciplines.

The creation of the multiple disciplines of social science was part of the general nineteenth-century attempt to secure and advance "objective" knowledge about "reality" on the basis of empirical findings (as opposed to "speculation"). The intent was to "learn" the truth, not invent or intuit it. The process of institutionalization of this kind of knowledge activity was not at all simple or straightforward. For one thing, it was not at first clear whether this activity was to be a singular one or should rather be divided into the several disciplines, as later occurred. Nor was it at the outset clear what was the best route to such knowledge, that is, what kind of epistemology would be most fruitful or even legitimate. Least of all was it clear whether the social sciences could in some sense be thought to constitute a "third culture" that was "between science and literature," in the later formulation of Wolf Lepenies. In fact, none of these questions has ever been definitively resolved. All we can do is to note the actual decisions that were made, or the majority positions that tended to prevail.

The first thing to note is where this institutionalization took place. There were five main locales for social science activity during the nineteenth century: Great Britain, France, the Germanies, the Italies, and the United States. Most of the scholars, most of the universities (of course, not all) were located in these five places. The universities in other countries lacked the numerical weight or international prestige of those in these five. To this day, most of the nineteenth-century works that we still read were written in one of these five locales.

*tending to Eurocentricity*

The second thing to note is that a very large and diverse set of names of "subject matters" or "disciplines" were put forward during the course of the century. However, by the First World War, there was general convergence or consensus around a few specific names, and the other candidates were more or less dropped. These names, as we shall discuss, were primarily five: history, economics, sociology, political science, and anthropology. One might add to this list, as we shall see, the so-called Oriental sciences (called Orientalism in English), despite the fact that they self-consciously did not consider themselves social sciences. Why we do not include geography, psychology, and law in this list we shall explain below.

The first of the social science disciplines to achieve an autonomous institutional existence was history. It is true that many historians vigorously rejected the label of social science, and some still do so today. We, however, regard the quarrels between the historians and the other social science disciplines as quarrels *within* social science, as we shall try to make clear as we proceed. History was of course a long-standing practice, and the term itself is ancient. Accounts of the past, particularly accounts of the past of one's own people, one's state, were a familiar activity in the world of knowledge. And hagiography had always been encouraged by those in power. What distinguished the new "discipline" of history, as it developed in the nineteenth century, was the rigorous emphasis it put on the search to find out *wie es eigentlich gewesen ist* ("what really happened"), in Ranke's famous phrase. As opposed to what? Most of all, as opposed to telling stories that were imagined or exaggerated, because they flattered the readers or served the immediate purposes of rulers or any other powerful groups.

It is hard to miss how much this Rankeian slogan reflected the themes used by "science" in its struggle with "philosophy"–the emphasis on the existence of a real world that is objective and knowable, the emphasis on empirical evidence, the emphasis on the neutrality of the scholar. Furthermore the historian, like the natural scientist, was not supposed to find his data in prior writings (the library, locus of reading) or in his own thought processes (the study, locus of reflection) but rather in a place where objective, external data could be assembled, stored, controlled, and manipulated (the laboratory / the archive, loci of research).

This common rejection of speculative philosophy drew history and science together as "modern" (that is, not medieval) modes of knowledge. But since the historians were also rejecting philosophy insofar as it entailed the search for general schemas which enabled one to explain empirical data, they felt that a search for scientific "laws" of the social world would only lead them back into error. It is this double meaning for historians of their rejection of philosophy that explains how they could in their work not only reflect the new dominance in European thought of the primacy of science but also be the strong heralds and proponents of an idiographic, antitheorizing stance. It is for this reason that, throughout the nineteenth century, most historians insisted that they belonged in faculties of letters and tended to be wary of any identification with the new category, the social sciences, that was slowly coming into fashion.

While it is true that some of the early nineteenth-century historians started out with some visions of a universal history (a last link with theology), the combination of their idiographic commitments and the social pressures coming from the states as well as from educated public opinion pushed historians in the direction of writing primarily their own national histories, the definition of the nation being more or less circumscribed by a push back in time of the space occupied in the present by the state boundaries in existence or in construction. In any case, the emphasis of historians on the use of archives, based on an in-depth contextual knowledge of the culture, made historical research seem most valid when performed in one's own backyard. Thus it was that historians, who had not wanted to engage any longer in justifying kings, found themselves engaged in justifying "nations" and often their new sovereigns, the "peoples."

This was no doubt useful to the states, but only indirectly, in

terms of reinforcing their social cohesion. It did not help them
to decide on wise policies in the present and certainly offered
little wisdom about the modalities of rational reformism. Between 1500 and 1800, the various states had already become ac-
customed to turning to specialists, often civil servants, to help
them forge policy, particularly in their mercantilist moments.
These specialists offered their knowledge under many rubrics,
such as jurisprudence (an old term) and law of the nations (a new
one), political economy (also a new term, indicating quite literally macroeconomics at the level of the polities), statistics (another new term, referring initially to quantitative data about the
states), and *Kameralwissenschaften* (administrative sciences).
Jurisprudence was already taught in the faculties of law of the
universities, and *Kameralwissenschaften* became a subject in
Germanic universities in the eighteenth century. However, only
in the nineteenth century do we begin to find a discipline called
economics, sometimes within the faculty of law, but often within
the faculty (sometimes ex-faculty) of philosophy. And given the
prevailing liberal economic theories of the nineteenth century,
the phrase "political economy" (popular in the eighteenth century) disappears in favor of "economics" by the second half of
the nineteenth century. By stripping away the adjective "political," economists could argue that economic behavior was the
reflection of a universal individualist psychology rather than of
socially constructed institutions, an argument which could then
be used to assert the naturalness of laissez-faire principles.

The universalizing assumptions of economics made the study
of economics very present oriented. As a result, economic history was always relegated to a minor place in economics curric-

ula, and the subdiscipline of economic history developed largely out of (and partially separated itself from) history more than out of economics. The one major attempt in the nineteenth century to develop a social science that was neither nomothetic nor idiographic but rather a search for the rules governing historically specific social systems was the construction in the Germanic zone of a field called *Staatswissenschaften*. This field covered (in present-day terms) a mixture of economic history, jurisprudence, sociology, and economics–insisting on the historical specificity of different "states" and making none of the disciplinary distinctions that were coming into use in Great Britain and France. The very name *Staatswissenschaften* ("sciences of the state") indicated that its proponents were seeking to occupy somewhat the same intellectual space that "political economy" had covered earlier in Great Britain and France, and therefore to serve the same function of providing knowledge that would be useful, at least in the longer run, to the states. This disciplinary invention flourished particularly in the second half of the nineteenth century but ultimately succumbed to attacks from without and cold feet from within. In the first decade of the twentieth century, German social science began to conform to the disciplinary categories in use in Great Britain and France. Some of the leading younger figures in *Staatswissenschaften*, such as Max Weber, took the lead in founding the German Sociological Society. By the 1920's, the term *Sozialwissenschaften* ("social sciences") had displaced *Staatswissenschaften*.

At the same time that economics was becoming an established discipline in the universities–present oriented and nomothetic–a totally new discipline was being invented, with an invented name: sociology. For the inventor, Comte, sociology was to be the queen of the sciences, an integrated and unified social science that was "positivist," another Comteian neologism. In practice, however, sociology as a discipline developed in the second half of the nineteenth century, principally out of the institutionalization and transformation within the universities of the work of social reform associations, whose agenda had been primarily that of dealing with the discontents and disorders of the much-enlarged urban working-class populations. By moving their work to a university setting, these social reformers largely surrendered their role of active, immediate legislative lobbying. But sociology has always nonetheless retained its concern with ordinary people and with the social consequences of modernity. Partly in order to consummate the break with its origins in social reform organizations, sociologists began to cultivate a positivist thrust, which, combined with their orientation toward the present, pushed them as well into the nomothetic camp.

Political science as a discipline emerged still later, not because its subject matter, the contemporary state and its politics, was less amenable to nomothetic analysis, but primarily because of the resistance of faculties of law to yield their monopoly in this arena. The resistance of law faculties may explain the importance given by political scientists to the study of political philosophy, sometimes under the name of political theory, at least up until the so-called behaviorist revolution of the post-1945 period. Political philosophy allowed the new discipline of political science to claim a heritage that went back to the Greeks and to read authors that had long had an assured place in university curricula.

Still, political philosophy was not enough to justify creating a new discipline; it could, after all, have continued to be taught within philosophy departments, and indeed it was. Political science as a separate discipline accomplished a further objective: it legitimated economics as a separate discipline. Political economy had been rejected as a subject matter because of the argument that the state and the market operated and should operate by distinctive logics. In the long run, this logically required as its guarantee the establishment of a separate scientific study of the political arena.

The quartet of history, economics, sociology, and political science, as they became university disciplines in the nineteenth century (and indeed right up to 1945), not only were practiced primarily in the five countries of their collective origin but were largely concerned with describing social reality in the same five countries. It is not that the universities of these five countries totally ignored the rest of the world. It is rather that they segregated their study into different disciplines.

The creation of the modern world-system involved the European encounter with, and in most cases conquest of, the peoples of the rest of the world. In terms of the categories of European experience, they encountered two rather different kinds of peoples and social structures. There were peoples who lived in relatively small groups, who had no system of written records, who did not seem to share in a geographically far-flung religious system, and who were militarily weak in relation to European technology. Generic terms to describe such peoples came into use: in English, they were usually called "tribes." In some other languages, they were called "races" (although this term later dropped out of use, because of its confusions with the other use of "races," referring to rather large groupings of human beings on the basis of skin color and other biological attributes). The study of these peoples became the domain of a new discipline called anthropology. As sociology had largely begun as the activity of social reform associations outside the universities, so had anthropology largely begun outside the university as a practice of explorers, travelers, and officials of the colonial services of the European powers. Like sociology, it subsequently became institutionalized as a university discipline, but one that was quite segregated from the other social sciences, which studied the Western world.

While some early anthropologists were attracted to the universal natural history of humankind (and its presumed stages of development), just as early historians were attracted to universal history, the social pressures of the external world pushed anthropologists into becoming ethnographers of particular peoples, usually chosen from among those found in the internal or external colonies of their country. This then almost inevitably implied a quite specific methodology, built around fieldwork (thereby meeting the requirement of the scientific ethos of empirical research) and participant observation in one particular area (meeting the requirement of achieving the in-depth knowledge of the culture required for understanding, so difficult to acquire in a culture very strange to the scientist).

Participant observation always threatened to violate the ideal of scientific neutrality, as did the temptation for the anthropologist (similar to that of the missionaries) to become a mediator for the people he/she studied with the European conquering

world, especially since the anthropologist tended to be a citizen
of the colonizing power of the people being studied (e.g., British
anthropologists in eastern and southern Africa, French anthropologists in West Africa, U.S. anthropologists in Guam or studying American Indians, Italian anthropologists in Libya). It was
their anchoring in the structures of the university that was most
influential in constraining anthropologists to maintain the practice of ethnography within the normative premises of science.
Furthermore, a search for the pristine "precontact" state of
cultures pushed ethnographers toward a belief that they were
dealing with "peoples without history," in Eric Wolf's pungent
formulation. This might have turned them toward a present-
oriented, nomothetic stance akin to economists, and after 1945
structural anthropology would take precisely this turn. But what
took priority initially was the need to justify the study of difference and to defend the moral legitimacy of not being European.
And therefore, following the same logic as that of the early historians, anthropologists resisted the demand to formulate laws,
practicing for the most part an idiographic epistemology.

All non-European peoples could not, however, be classified as
"tribes." Europeans had long had contact with other so-called
"high civilizations," such as the Arab-Islamic world and China.
These zones were considered "high" civilizations by Europeans
precisely because they did have writing, did have religious systems that were geographically widespread, and were organized
politically (at least for long stretches of time) in the form of
large, bureaucratic empires. European study of these civilizations had begun with the medieval clerics. Between the thir-
teenth and the eighteenth centuries, these "civilizations" were
still militarily sufficiently resistant to European conquest that

they merited respect, even sometimes admiration, and yet, to be sure, puzzlement as well.

In the nineteenth century, however, as a result of Europe's further technological advances, these "civilizations" were made into European colonies, or at least into semicolonies. Oriental studies, whose original home was in the Church and whose original justification was as an auxiliary to evangelization, became a more secular practice, eventually finding a place in the evolving disciplinary structures of the universities. The institutionalization of Oriental studies was in fact preceded by that of the ancient Mediterranean world, what in English was called the "classics," the study of Europe's own antiquity. This was also a study of a civilization that was different from that of modern Europe, but it was not treated in the same way as Oriental studies. Rather it was considered to be the history of those peoples who were defined as the ancestors of modern Europe, unlike, say, the study of ancient Egypt or of Mesopotamia. The civilization of antiquity was explicated as the early phase of a single continuous historical development that culminated in modern "Western" civilization. It was thus seen as part of a single saga: first antiquity, then with barbarian conquest the continuity provided by the Church, then with the Renaissance the reincorporation of the Greco-Roman heritage and the creation of the modern world. In this sense, antiquity had no autonomous history; rather, it constituted the prologue of modernity. By contrast, but following the same logic, the other "civilizations" had no autonomous history either; rather, they became the story of histories that were frozen, that had not progressed, that had not culminated in modernity.

Classics was primarily a literary study, although it obviously overlapped with the historical study of Greece and Rome. In seeking to create a discipline separate from philosophy (and theology), the classicists defined their subject matter as a combination of all kinds of literature (not merely the kind which philosophers recognized), the arts (and its new adjunct, archaeology), and such history as could be done in the mode of the new history (which was not too much, given the paucity of primary sources). This combination made classics close in practice to the simultaneously emerging disciplines that focused on the national literatures of each of the major Western European states.

The bellettristic tone of classics set the scene for the many varieties of Oriental studies that began to enter the university curricula. Given their premises, however, Orientalist scholars adopted a very special practice. What became of interest was not reconstructing diachronic sequences, as for European history, since this history was not presumed to progress. What was of interest was understanding and appreciating the set of values and practices that created civilizations which, although considered to be "high" civilizations, were nonetheless thought to be immobile. Such understanding could best be achieved, it was argued, by a close reading of the texts that incarnated their wisdom; and this required linguistic and philological skills, quite akin to those that had been traditionally used by the monks in the study of Christian texts. In this sense, Oriental studies resisted modernity altogether and was not therefore caught up for the most part in the scientific ethos. Even more than the historians, the Orientalist scholars saw no virtue in social science, and rigorously shunned association with the domain, preferring to consider themselves part of the "humanities." Still, they filled an important niche in the social sciences since, for a long time, Orientalist scholars were virtually the only ones in the university who engaged in the study of social realities that related to China, or India, or Persia. There were, to be sure, in addition a few social scientists who were interested in comparing Oriental civilizations with Western civilizations (such as Max Weber, Arnold Toynbee, and, less systematically, Karl Marx). But these comparativist scholars, unlike the Orientalist scholars, were not concerned with Oriental civilizations for their own sake. Rather, their primary intellectual concern was always to explain why it was the Western world, and not these other civilizations, that went forward to modernity (or capitalism).

A word needs to be said as well of three fields that never quite made it as principal components of the social sciences: geography, psychology, and law. Geography, like history, was an ancient practice. In the late nineteenth century, it reconstructed itself as a new discipline, primarily in German universities, which served to inspire developments elsewhere. While the concerns of geography were primarily those of a social science, it resisted categorization. It sought to bridge the gap with the natural sciences through its concern with physical geography, as well as with the humanities through its concern with what was called human geography (in some ways doing work similar to that of anthropologists, though with an emphasis on environmental influences). Furthermore, geography was the one discipline in the period before 1945 that in practice consciously tried to be truly worldwide in terms of its subject matter. This was its virtue and perhaps its undoing. As the study of social reality became increasingly compartmentalized in the late nineteenth century into separate disciplines, with a clear division of labor, geography appeared anachronistic in its generalist, synthesizing, nonanalytic penchants.

Probably in consequence, geography remained through all this period a sort of poor relation in terms of numbers and prestige, often serving merely as a kind of minor adjunct to history. As a result, treatment of space and place was relatively neglected in the social sciences. The focus on progress and the politics of organizing social change made the temporal dimension of social existence crucial, but left the spatial dimension in limbo. If processes were universal and deterministic, space was theoretically irrelevant. If processes verged on being unique and unrepeatable, space became merely one element (and a minor one) of specificity. In the former view, space was seen as merely a platform upon which events unfolded or processes operated – essentially inert, just there and no more. In the latter view, space became a context influencing events (in idiographic history, in realist international relations, in "neighborhood effects," even in Marshallian externalities). But for the most part, these contextual effects were seen as mere influences – residuals that had to be taken into account to get better empirical results, but ones that were not central to the analysis.

Nonetheless, social science in practice based itself on a particular view of spatiality, albeit one that was unavowed. The set of spatial structures through which social scientists assumed lives were organized were the sovereign territories that collectively defined the world political map. Nearly all social scientists assumed that these political boundaries fixed the spatial parameters of other key interactions – the sociologist's society, the macroeconomist's national economy, the political scientist's polity, the historian's nation. Each assumed a fundamental spatial congruence between political, social, and economic processes. In this sense, social science was very much a creature, if not a creation, of the states, taking their boundaries as crucial social containers.

Psychology was a different case. Here too, the discipline separated out of philosophy, seeking to reconstitute itself in the new scientific form. Its practice, however, came to be defined as lying not in the social arena but primarily in the medical arena, which meant that its legitimacy depended on the closeness of its association with the natural sciences. Furthermore, the positivists, sharing the premise of Comte ("the eye cannot look at itself"), pushed psychology in this direction. For many, the only psychology that could be scientifically legitimate would be one that was physiological, even chemical. Hence these psychologists sought to move "beyond" social science to become a "biological" science, and consequently in most universities psychology eventually shifted its berth from faculties of the social sciences to those of the natural sciences.

There were, of course, forms of psychological theorizing which placed their emphasis on the analysis of the individual in society. These so-called social psychologists did try to remain within the camp of social science. But social psychology was for the most part not successful in establishing a full institutional autonomy, and suffered vis-à-vis psychology the same kind of marginalization that economic history suffered vis-à-vis economics. In many cases, it survived by being absorbed as a subdiscipline within sociology. There were, to be sure, various kinds of psychology that were not positivistic: for example, *geisteswis-senschaftliche* psychology and *Gestalt* psychology.

The strongest and most influential theorizing in psychology that might have turned it toward defining itself as a social science, Freudian theory, failed to do so for two reasons. First, it emerged out of medical practice, and second, its initially scandalous quality made it, as an activity, something of a pariah, leading psychoanalysts to create structures of institutional reproduction totally outside the university system. This may have preserved psychoanalysis as a practice and a school of thought, but it meant that within the university Freudian concepts found their berth largely in departments other than psychology.

Legal studies was a third field that never quite became a social science. For one thing, there already was a faculty of law, and its curricula was closely linked to its primary function of training lawyers. The nomothetic social scientists regarded jurisprudence with some skepticism. It seemed too normative, too little rooted in empirical investigation. Its laws were not scientific laws. Its context seemed too idiographic. Political science broke away from analysis of such laws and their history in order to analyze the abstract rules which governed political behavior, from which it would be possible to derive appropriately rational legal systems.

There is one last aspect of the institutionalization of social science that is important to note. The process took place at the very time that Europe was finally confirming its dominion over the rest of the world. This gave rise to the obvious question: why was this small part of the world able to defeat all rivals and impose its will on the Americas, Africa, and Asia? This was a very big question, and most answers to it were offered not at the level of the sovereign states but at the level of comparative "civilizations" (to which we have adverted previously). It was Europe as "Western" civilization that had demonstrated superior productive and military prowess, not just Great Britain or France or Germany, whatever the sizes of their individual empires. This concern with how Europe expanded to dominate the world coincided with the Darwinian intellectual transition. The secularization of knowledge promoted by the Enlightenment was confirmed by the theory of evolution, and Darwinian theories spread far beyond their biological origins. Although Newtonian physics as exemplar dominated social science methodology, Darwinian biology had a very great influence on social theorizing through the seemingly irresistible meta-construct of evolution, with a great deal of emphasis on the concept of the survival of the fittest.

The concept of the survival of the fittest was subject to much use and abuse, and was often confused with the concept of success through competition. A loose interpretation of evolutionary theory could be used to provide scientific legitimation to the assumption that progress culminated in the self-evident superiority of contemporary European society: stage theories of societal development culminating in industrial civilization, Whig interpretations of history, climatological determinism, Spencerian sociology. These early studies in comparative civilization were, however, not as state-centric as fully institutionalized social science. They thus fell victim to the impact of the two world wars, which together undermined some of the liberal optimism upon which the progressive theories of civilizations were built. Hence in the twentieth century history, anthropology, and geography finally marginalized completely what remained of their earlier universalizing traditions, and the state-centric trinity of sociology, economics, and political science consolidated their positions as the core (nomothetic) social sciences.

Thus, between 1850 and 1945, a series of disciplines came to be defined as constituting an arena of knowledge to which the name "social science" was accorded. This was done by establishing in the principal universities first chairs, then departments offering courses leading to degrees in the discipline. The institutionalization of training was accompanied by the institutionalization of research: the creation of journals specialized in each of the disciplines; the construction of associations of scholars along disciplinary lines (first national, then international); the creation of library collections catalogued by disciplines.

An essential element in this process of institutionalizing the disciplines was the effort by each of them to define what distinguished each from the other, especially what differentiated each from those that seemed closest in content in the study of social realities. Beginning with Leopold von Ranke, Barthold Niebuhr, and Johann Droysen, historians asserted their special relationship to a special type of materials, especially archival sources and similar texts. They stressed that they were interested in reconstructing past reality by relating it to the cultural needs of the present, in an interpretative and hermeneutic way, insisting on studying phenomena, even the most complex ones like whole cultures or nations, as individualities and as moments (or parts) of diachronic and synchronic contexts.

Anthropologists reconstructed modes of social organization

of peoples that were quite different from the Western forms. They demonstrated that customs strange to Western eyes were not irrational, but functioned to preserve and reproduce populations. Orientalist scholars studied, explicated, and translated the texts of non-Western "high" civilizations and were instrumental in legitimating the concept of "world religions," which was a break with Christocentric views.

Most of the nomothetic social sciences stressed first what differentiated them from the historical discipline: an interest in arriving at general laws that were presumed to govern human behavior, a readiness to perceive the phenomena to be studied as cases (not individualities), the need to segmentalize human reality in order to analyze it, the possibility and desirability of strict scientific methods (such as theory-related formulation of hypotheses to be tested against evidence via strict, and if possible quantitative, procedures), a preference for systematically produced evidence (e.g., survey data) and controlled observations over received texts and other residuals.

Once social science was distinguished in this way from idiographic history, the nomothetic social scientists–economists, political scientists, and sociologists–were also anxious to stake out their separate terrains as essentially different one from the other (both in subject matter and in methodology). Economists did this by insisting on the validity of a *ceteris paribus* assumption in studying market operations. Political scientists did it by restricting their concerns to formal governmental structures. Sociologists did it by insisting on an emergent social terrain ignored by the economists and the political scientists.

All this, it may be said, was largely a success story. The estab-

lishment of the disciplinary structures created viable, productive structures of research, analysis, and training, which gave
birth to the considerable literature that today we consider the
heritage of contemporary social science. By 1945, the panoply of
disciplines comprising the social sciences was basically institutionalized in most of the major universities of the world. There
had been resistance to (indeed, often refusal of) these classifications in the fascist and communist countries. With the end of
the Second World War, German and Italian institutions fell into
line fully with the accepted pattern, and the Soviet-bloc countries did so by the late 1950's. Furthermore, by 1945 the social
sciences were clearly distinguished on the one hand from the
natural sciences, which studied nonhuman systems, and on the
other from the humanities, which studied the cultural, mental,
and spiritual production of "civilized" human societies.

After the Second World War, however, at the very moment
when the institutional structures of the social sciences seemed
for the first time fully in place and clearly delineated, the practices of social scientists began to change. This was to create a
gap, one that would grow, between the practices and intellectual
positions of social scientists on the one side and the formal organization of the social sciences on the other.

# II. Debates Within the Social Sciences, 1945 to the Present

> Disciplines constitute a system of control in the production of discourse, fixing its limits through the action of an identity taking the form of a permanent reactivation of the rules.
>
> —Michel Foucault[7]

Three developments after 1945 profoundly affected the structure of the social sciences that had been put into place in the preceding hundred years. The first was the change in the world political structure. The United States emerged from the Second World War with overwhelming economic strength, within a world that was politically defined by two new geopolitical realities: the so-called cold war between the United States and the U.S.S.R., and the historical reassertion of the non-European peoples of the world. The second development was the fact that, in the twenty-five years following 1945, the world had the largest expansion of its productive capacity and population that it had ever known, one that involved an expansion in scale of all human activities. The third was the consequent extraordinary quantitative and geographic expansion of the univer-

7. Michel Foucault, *The Archaeology of Knowledge and the Discourse on Language* (New York: Pantheon, 1972), p. 224.

sity system everywhere in the world, which led to a multiplication of the numbers of professional social scientists. Each of these three new social realities posed a problem for the social sciences, as they had been historically institutionalized.

The enormous strength of the U.S. vis-à-vis all other states affected profoundly the definition of what were the most urgent issues to be addressed, and what were the most suitable ways of addressing them. The overwhelming economic advantage of the U.S. in the fifteen to twenty-five years following the Second World War meant that, for a while at least, social scientific activity was located primarily within U.S. institutions to an unusual degree, and this of course affected how priorities were defined by social scientists. On the other hand, the political reassertion of the non-European peoples meant that many assumptions of social science would be called into question on the grounds that they reflected the political biases of an era which was now over, or at least ending.

The runaway expansion of the university system worldwide had a very specific organizational implication. It created a structural pressure for increased specialization simply because scholars were in search of niches that could define their originality or at least their social utility. The most immediate effect was to encourage reciprocal intrusions by social scientists into neighboring disciplinary domains, ignoring in the process the various legitimations that each of the social sciences had erected to justify their specificities as reserved realms. And the economic expansion fueled this specialization by providing the resources that made it possible.

There was a second organizational implication. The world

economic expansion involved a quantum leap in scale–for the state machineries and for the economic enterprises, to be sure, but also for the organizations of research. The major powers, largely stimulated by the cold war, began to invest in big science, and this investment was extended to the social sciences. The percentage allocated to the social sciences was small, but the absolute figures were very high in relation to anything that had previously been available. This economic input encouraged a further, fuller scientization of the social sciences. The result was the emergence of centralized poles of scientific development with a concentration of information and skill, with financial resources that were provided primarily by the U.S. and other major states, by foundations (largely U.S. based), but also, to a lesser extent, by transnational corporations.

Wherever the institutional structuring of the social sciences was incomplete, U.S. scholars and institutions encouraged, directly and indirectly, following the established model, with particular emphasis on the more nomothetic tendencies within the social sciences. The massive public and private investment in scientific research gave these poles of scientific development an unquestionable advantage over orientations that seemed less rigorous and policy oriented. Thus, the economic expansion reinforced the worldwide legitimation within social science of the scientific paradigms that underlay the technological achievements behind it. At the same time, however, the ending of the political dominion of the Western world over the rest of the world meant that new voices were entering the scene not only of politics but also of social science.

We shall discuss the consequences of these changes in the

world for three successive issues: (1) the validity of the distinctions among the social sciences; (2) the degree to which the heritage is parochial; (3) the utility and reality of the distinction between the "two cultures."

## 1. The Validity of the Distinctions among the Social Sciences

There were three clear lines of cleavage in the system of disciplines erected to structure the social sciences in the late nineteenth century: the line between the study of the modern/civilized world (history plus the three nomothetic social sciences) and the study of the nonmodern world (anthropology, plus Oriental studies); within the study of the modern world, the line between the past (history) and the present (the nomothetic social sciences); within the nomothetic social sciences, the sharp lines between the study of the market (economics), the state (political science), and civil society (sociology). Each of these lines of cleavage came to be challenged in the post-1945 world.

Probably the most notable academic innovation after 1945 was the creation of area studies as a new institutional category to group intellectual work. This concept first emerged in the United States during the Second World War. It was widely implemented in the United States in the ten years following the end of the war, and it subsequently spread to universities in other parts of the world. The basic idea of area studies was very simple. An area was a large geographic zone which had some supposed cultural, historic, and often linguistic coherence. The list as it emerged was very heterodox in character: the U.S.S.R., China (or East Asia), Latin America, the Middle East, Africa, South

Asia, Southeast Asia, East-Central Europe, and, much later, Western Europe as well. In some countries, the United States (or North America) also became the object of area studies. Not every university adopted exactly these geographic categories, of course. There were many variations.

Area studies was supposed to be an arena of both scholarship and pedagogy, one which brought together all those persons– primarily from the various social sciences, but often from the humanities as well, and occasionally even from some natural sciences–on the basis of a shared interest in doing work in their discipline about the given "area" (or a part of it). Area studies was by definition "multidisciplinary." The political motivations underlying its origins were quite explicit. The United States, given its worldwide political role, needed knowledge about, and therefore specialists on, the current realities of these various regions, especially since these regions were now becoming so politically active. Area studies programs were designed to train such specialists, as were subsequent parallel programs first in the U.S.S.R. and in western Europe, and then in many other parts of the world (e.g., Japan, India, Australia, and various Latin American countries).

Area studies brought within a single structure (at least for part of their intellectual life) persons whose disciplinary affiliations cut across the three cleavages we have mentioned: the historians and nomothetic social scientists found themselves face to face with the anthropologists and the Orientalist scholars, the historians face to face with the nomothetic social scientists, and each type of nomothetic social scientist with the others. In addition, there were occasionally geographers, art historians, students of national literatures, epidemiologists, even geologists. These people constructed curricula together, sat on the doctoral committees of each other's students, attended conferences of area specialists, read each other's books, and published in new transdisciplinary journals specializing in the areas.

Whatever the intellectual value of this cross-fertilization, the organizational consequences for the social sciences were immense. Although area studies was presented in the restricted guise of multidisciplinarity (a concept that had already been under discussion in the interwar period), its practice exposed the fact that there was considerable artificiality in the sharp institutional separations of social science knowledge. Historians and nomothetic social scientists were for the first time (at least in any numbers) engaging in the study of non-Western areas. This intrusion into the non-Western world of disciplines previously oriented to the study of the Western world undermined the logic of the previous arguments justifying separate arenas called ethnography and Oriental studies. It seemed to imply that the methods and the models of history and the nomothetic social sciences were applicable to non-Western regions as well as to Europe and North America. Within two decades, anthropologists began to renounce ethnography as their defining activity, seeking alternative justifications for their field. Orientalist scholars went further; they surrendered their very name, merging themselves variously into departments of history, philosophy, classics, and religion, as well as into newly created departments of regional cultural studies that covered contemporary cultural production as well as the texts Orientalist scholars had traditionally studied.

Area studies affected the structure of the departments of history and the three nomothetic social sciences as well. By the 1960's, a significant number of members of the faculty of these departments had become committed to doing their empirical work on non-Western areas of the world. The percentage was largest in history, smallest in economics, with political science and sociology somewhere in between. This meant that internal discussions within these disciplines were inevitably affected by the fact that the data they were debating, the courses they were asking students to take, and the subjects of legitimate research had become considerably wider in geographical terms. When we add to this geographic expansion of the subject matter the geographic expansion of the source of recruitment of the scholars, the social situation within the institutions of knowledge may be said to have undergone a significant evolution in the post-1945 period.

The disintegration of the intellectual segregation between the study of Western and non-Western areas posed a fundamental intellectual question, with some larger political implications. Were the two zones ontologically identical or different? The predominant previous assumption had been that they were sufficiently different that they required different social science disciplines to study them. Was one now to make the opposite assumption, that there was no difference of any kind that would warrant some special form of analysis for the non-Western world? The nomothetic social scientists debated whether the generalizations (laws) that they had been establishing were equally applicable to the study of non-Western areas. For more idiographic historians, the debate was posed as the question, one that was seriously asked: does Africa have a history? or do only "historic nations" have histories?

The intellectual response to these queries was essentially an uncertain compromise. It might be summarized as the argument that non-Western areas were analytically the same as Western areas, but not quite! The primary form that this argument took was modernization theory. It of course built on many discussions and premises (explicit and implicit) in the earlier social science literature, but nonetheless modernization literature took a particular form and became very important in social science theorizing. The key thesis was that there exists a common modernizing path of all nations/peoples/areas (hence they were the same) but that nations/peoples/areas find themselves at different stages on this path (hence they were not quite the same). In terms of public policy, this was translated into a worldwide concern with "development," a term that was defined as the process by which a country advanced along the universal path of modernization. Organizationally, the concern with modernization/development tended to bring the multiple social sciences together in common projects, and in a common stance vis-à-vis public authorities. The political commitment of the states to development became one of the great justifications for expending public funds on research by social scientists.

Modernization/development had the characteristic that this model could be applied to Western zones as well, by interpreting the historical development of the Western world as the progressive and precocious achievement of modernization. This provided a basis on which the previously present-oriented nomothetic social scientists began to find a justification for using data that were not contemporary, despite the fact that such data were more incomplete, while historians began to consider whether some of the generalizations put forth by nomothetic social scientists might not help to elucidate their understanding (even their hermeneutic understanding) of the past. The attempt to bridge the gap between idiographic history and nomothetic social science did not begin in 1945. It has an earlier trajectory. The movement called "new history" in the United States in the early twentieth century and the movements in France (*Annales* and its predecessors) were explicitly such attempts. However, only in the post-1945 period did such attempts begin to attract substantial support among historians.

Indeed, it was only in the 1960's that the quest for close cooperation and even mixing between (parts of) history and (parts of) the social sciences became a very noticeable and noted phenomenon. In history, the conviction gained some ground that the received profile of the discipline no longer fully served modern needs. Historians had been better in studying past politics than past social and economic life. Historical studies had tended to concentrate on events, and on the motives of individuals and institutions, and they had been less well equipped for analyzing the more anonymous processes and structures that were located in the *longue durée*. Structures and processes seemed to have been neglected. All this was to be changed by broadening the scope of historical studies: by adding more economic and social history, in its own right, and as a key to understanding history in general.

Fundamental changes in the discipline of history were advocated, with the help of the neighboring social sciences. The social sciences had tools to offer in the study of dimensions of the past that were "beneath" or "behind" historical institutions, events, and ideas (dimensions such as economic change, population growth, social inequality and mobility, mass attitudes and behavior, social protest, and voting patterns), tools that the historians did not possess: quantitative methods; analytic concepts like class, role expectations, or status discrepancy; models of social change. Some historians sought now to use such "mass data" as marriage registers, election results, and tax documents, and for this the turn to the social sciences proved indispensable. As history (and anthropology) became more open to quantitative research, there was a process of circular reinforcement: money, numbers of scholars, and social legitimacy all fed each other, and strengthened the sense of self-confidence in the intellectual warranty of the conceptual constructs of social science.

Sometimes the quest for change in the discipline of history went hand in hand with a desire to engage in social and cultural criticism. It was argued that the historians had overstressed consensus and the functioning of institutions and had underestimated conflict, deprivation, and inequalities of class, ethnicity, and gender. Criticism of the received paradigms combined with challenges to established authorities inside and outside the profession. Sometimes, as in Germany, such a revisionist mood reinforced the turn of historians toward the social sciences. Using analytical concepts and theoretical approaches was in itself a way of expressing opposition to the established "historicist" paradigm, which stressed hermeneutic approaches and language as close to the sources as possible. Some social science traditions seemed to offer specific tools for developing a "critical" history, or rather a "critical historical social science." But in other countries, like the U.S., which not only had other, less "historicist" traditions in history but also a less critical tradition in the social sciences, radical revisionist historians felt less attracted by social science approaches.

Economics, sociology, and political science flourished in the postwar period, in part basking in the reflection of the glories of the natural sciences, and their high prestige and influence were another reason why many historians found it interesting to draw on their work. At the same time, some social scientists were beginning to move into realms previously reserved to the historians. This expansion of the nomothetic social sciences into history took, however, two quite different forms. On the one hand, there was the application of relatively specific and narrow social science theories, models, and procedures to data about the past (sometimes even from the past)—for example, studies on voting patterns, social mobility, and economic growth. Such data were treated like other variables or indicators in the empirical social sciences, that is, they were standardized (in time series), isolated, and correlated. This was sometimes called "social science history." These social scientists were expanding the loci from which they drew their data, but they did not think it necessary or desirable to change their procedures in any way; they certainly did not become traditional historians. Most of them neither expected nor found much that was different about the past. Data about the past seemed rather to corroborate or at most modify slightly the general laws in which they were basically interested. Still, sometimes the results of such work became very important for historians and contributed to a better understanding on their part of the past.

There was, however, a quite different turn toward history on the part of some other social scientists, those who were interested in describing and explaining large-scale social change, sometimes in a Weberian, sometimes in a Marxian tradition, often somewhere in between. They produced various types of what came to be called "historical sociology." They were critical of the ahistoricism of their colleagues, who they felt had lost touch with many of the best earlier traditions in the social sciences. The work they did was less "scientistic" and more "historicist." They took specific historical contexts seriously and placed social change into the center of the story they told. Their works did not aim primarily at testing, modifying, and formulating laws (for example, of modernization), but rather used general rules to explain complex and changing phenomena or interpret them in the light of those general patterns. In the 1960's, this criticism of ahistoricism began to be increasingly expressed by younger social scientists as they turned to social criticism. Their criticism of "mainstream" social sciences included the assertion that they had neglected the centrality of social change, favoring a mythology of consensus, and that they showed a naive, even arrogant, self-assuredness in applying Western concepts to the analysis of very different phenomena and cultures.

In the case of "social science history," social scientists were moving toward history as a consequence of the logic and the expansive dynamics of their disciplines. They were seeking less to "bridge the gap" with history than to acquire larger data bases. This was not true of the "historical sociologists," whose work involved a critique of prevailing methodologies. A similar motive was at play among many of the historians who were calling for the use of social scientific techniques and generalizations. There was a convergence of the writings of the historical (or historicizing) social scientists with those of the "structuralist" historians, which seemed to hit its stride in the 1970's, although there usually still remained certain differences in style: proximity to the sources, level of generalization, the degree of narrative presentation, and even footnoting techniques.

This move toward a closer cooperation between history and the other social sciences remained, nonetheless, a minority phenomenon. Furthermore, in addition to the history-sociology discussion, there seemed to be separate ones between history and each of the other social sciences: economics (e.g., the "new economic history"), political science (e.g., the "new institutionalism"), anthropology ("historical anthropology"), and geography ("historical geography"). In all of these fields, some of this convergence came about in the form of simple expansion of the data domain of a particular social science tradition, and some of it took the form of the reopening of fundamental methodological issues.

The growing overlap among the three traditional nomothetic social sciences—economics, political science, and sociology—was less charged with controversy. The sociologists led the way, making both "political sociology" and "economic sociology" into important and standard subfields within the discipline as early as the 1950's. The political scientists followed suit. They expanded their concerns beyond formal governmental institutions, redefining their subject matter to include all social processes that had political implications or intentions: the study of pressure groups, protest movements, community organizations. And when some critical social scientists revived the use of the term "political economy," other, less critical political scientists responded by trying to give the term and the subject matter a more classically nomothetic flavor. The common result, however, was to engage the political scientists in a fuller concern with economic processes. For the economists, the early postwar dominance of Keynesian ideas revived concern with "macroeconomics," whereupon the dividing line with political science became less clear, since the object of analysis was largely the policies of governments and intergovernmental agencies. Later on, some non-Keynesian economists began to argue the merits of using neoclassical economic analytic models for the study of subjects traditionally considered sociological, such as the family or social deviance.

All three disciplines were increasing the degree of their commitment to quantitative techniques and even mathematical modeling in the early postwar years; as a result, the distinctiveness of their methodological approaches seemed to diminish. When social criticism began to fuel the internal debates of these disciplines, the limitations that the critical social scientists in each discipline found in the positivist doctrines prevailing in their discipline seemed about the same in each. Once again, there is no point in exaggerating. Organizationally the three disciplines remained quite distinct, and there was no lack of voices to defend this separation. However, over the years, in the case of both the mainstream and the critical versions of each, there began to be in practice an increasing overlap in subject matter and methodology among the three nomothetic disciplines.

The multiple overlaps between the disciplines had a double consequence. Not only did it become less and less simple to find clear, distinguishing lines between them in terms of either the domain of concern or the ways in which the data were treated, but each discipline also became more and more heterogeneous because of stretching the boundaries of acceptable subjects of inquiry. This led to considerable internal questioning about the coherence of the disciplines and the legitimacy of the intellectual premises each had used to argue for its right to a separate existence. One way of handling this was the attempt to create new "interdisciplinary" names, like communications studies, administrative sciences, and behavioral sciences.

Many consider the growing emphasis on multidisciplinarity as the expression of a flexible response by the social sciences to problems encountered and intellectual objections raised to the structuring of the disciplines. They feel that the convergence of parts of the social sciences and parts of history toward a more comprehensive social science has been a creative approach that has involved a fruitful cross-fertilization and deserves to be further advanced and developed. Others feel less sanguine about what has been achieved. They believe that the concession of "interdisciplinarity" has served as much to salvage the legitimacy of the existing disciplines as to overcome the waning logic of their distinctiveness. The latter have urged a more radical reconstruction to overcome what they perceive as intellectual confusion.

However one appreciates the very clear trend to the theme of multidisciplinarity, the organizational consequences seem evident. Whereas the number of names used to classify social science knowledge activity had been steadily reduced between 1850 and 1945, ending up with a relatively small list of accepted names for disciplines, the period after 1945 saw the curve move in the reverse direction, with new names constantly coming into existence and finding appropriate institutional bases: new programs or even new departments within the university, new scholarly associations, new journals, and new categories in the classification of books in libraries.

The validity of the distinctions among the social sciences was probably the major focus of critical debate in the 1950's and 1960's. Towards the end of the 1960's, and then very clearly in the 1970's, two other questions that had arisen in the postwar period came to the fore: the degree to which social science (indeed all of knowledge) was "Eurocentric" and therefore the degree to which the social science heritage could be considered parochial; and the degree to which the encrusted division of modern thought into the "two cultures" was a useful mode of organizing intellectual activity. It is to these two questions that we now turn.

## 2. The Degree to Which the Heritage Is Parochial

The claim to universality, however qualified–universal relevance, universal applicability, universal validity–is inherent in the justification of all academic disciplines. That is part of the requirement for their institutionalization. The justification may be made on moral, practical, aesthetic, or political grounds, or some combination thereof, but all institutionalized knowledge proceeds on the presumption that the lessons of the case at hand have significant bearing on the next case, and that the list of potential cases is, for all practical purposes, endless. To be sure, any such contentions are rarely convincing once and for all. The three major divisions of contemporary knowledge (the humanities, the natural sciences, and the social sciences), as well as the disciplines considered to be located within each of them, have all struggled continuously on a number of different fronts—intellectual, ideological, and political—to maintain their various claims to universality. This is because all such claims are of course historically specific, conceivable only from within a particular social system, always enforced through historical, and therefore perishable, institutions and practices.

The universalism of any discipline or larger grouping of disciplines rests on a particular and changing mix of intellectual claims and social practices. These claims and practices feed on each other and are, in turn, enhanced by the institutional reproduction of the discipline or division. Change takes most often the form of adaptation, a continuous fine tuning of both the universal lessons supposedly transmitted and the ways in which they are transmitted. Historically, this has meant that once a discipline was institutionalized, its universalist claims have been hard to challenge successfully regardless of their current intellectual plausibility.

The expectation of universality, however sincerely pursued, has not been fulfilled thus far in the historical development of the social sciences. In recent years, critics have been severe in their denunciations of the failures and inadequacies of the social sciences in this pursuit. The more extreme of the critics have suggested that universality is an unrealizable objective. But most social scientists still believe it is a worthy and plausible objective, even if up to now social science has been unacceptably parochial. Some would argue that the recent criticisms made by groups previously excluded from the world of social science itself creates the conditions that will make true universalism possible.

In many ways, the most severe problems have been with the three more nomothetic social sciences. In taking the natural sciences as a model, they nurtured three kinds of expectations that have proved impossible to fulfill as stated in universalist form: an expectation of prediction; an expectation of management; both in turn premised on an expectation of quantifiable accuracy. Whereas matters of debate in the domain carved by the humanities were sometimes thought to rest on the subjective preferences of the researcher, the nomothetic social sciences built themselves on the premises that social achievement can be measured, and that the measurements themselves can be agreed upon universally.

The wager that nomothetic social science could produce universal knowledge was in fact, we see in retrospect, quite risky. For, unlike the natural world as defined by the natural sciences, the domain of the social sciences not only is one in which the object of study encompasses the researchers themselves but also is one in which the persons they study can enter into dialogues or contests of various kinds with these researchers. Matters of debate in the natural sciences are normally solved without recourse to the opinions of the object of study. In contrast, the peoples (or their descendants) studied by social scientists have entered increasingly into the discussion, whether or not their opinion was sought by scholars, who, indeed, frequently considered this intrusion unwelcome. The intrusion has increasingly taken the form of a challenge to universalist pretensions. Dissident voices–notably (but not only) feminists–have questioned the ability of the social sciences to account for their reality. They seem to have been telling the researchers: "Your analysis may have been appropriate for your group. It simply does not fit our case." Or even more sweepingly, the dissidents have questioned the very principle of universalism. They have alleged that what the social sciences presented as applicable to the whole world represented in fact the views of a minuscule minority within humankind. Furthermore, they argued, the views of that minority had come to dominate the world of knowledge, simply because the same minority was also dominant in the world outside the universities.

Skepticism about the virtues of the social sciences as unbiased interpretations of the human world preceded their institutionalization and surfaced in the works of prominent Western intellectuals from Herder and Rousseau to Marx and Weber. In many ways, the current denunciations of these disciplines as Eurocentric/masculinist/bourgeois endeavors are, to some extent, merely a repetition of earlier criticisms, both implicit and explicit, by practitioners and outsiders alike, but the earlier criticisms were largely ignored.

It is hardly surprising that the social sciences constructed in Europe and North America in the nineteenth century were Eurocentric. The European world of the time felt itself culturally triumphant, and in many ways it was. Europe had conquered the world, both politically and economically. Its technological achievements were an essential element in this conquest, and it seemed logical to ascribe the superior technology to a superior science, a superior worldview. It seemed plausible to identify the European achievement with the thrust toward universal progress. The period of the two world wars was a first shock, seeming to belie Western claims to moral progress, but in 1945 the Western world took heart again. It is only when the political dominance of the West began to be significantly challenged after 1945, and when East Asia became a new, very powerful locus of economic activity in the 1970's, that the challenge to the cultural universality of Western ideas began to be taken seriously. Moreover, this challenge was being made not merely by those who felt left out in the analyses of social science but within Western social science as well. The self-doubts of the West, which had existed only among a small minority before, now loomed much larger.

It is thus within the context of changes in the distribution of power in the world that the issue of the cultural parochialism of the social sciences as they had historically developed came to the fore. It represented the civilizational correlate to the loss of unquestioned political and economic dominance by the West in the world arena. The civilizational question did not, however, take the form of a straightforward conflict. Attitudes were deeply ambiguous, and neither Western nor non-Western scholars formed groups that had a unified position on this question (*a fortiori* one in opposition to that of the other group). Organizationally, the links between them were complex. Many non-Western scholars had been trained in Western universities, and many more considered themselves committed to epistemologies, methodologies, and theorizing associated with Western scholars. Conversely, there were some Western scholars, to be sure few in

number, who were profoundly cognizant of the current thinking of non-Western social scientists and were deeply influenced by it.

On the whole, in the period from 1945 to 1970 the social scientific views that were dominant in Europe and North America
remained dominant in the non-Western world as well. Indeed,
this period was one in which social science scholarship expanded considerably in the non-Western world, often under the
aegis of or with the help of Western institutions, which preached
the acceptance of the disciplines as they had developed in the
West as being universally normative. Social scientists, no less
than political or religious leaders, have missions; they seek the
universal acceptance of certain practices in the belief that this
will maximize the possibility of achieving certain ends, such as
knowing the truth. Under the banner of the universality of
science, they seek to define the forms of knowledge that are
scientifically legitimate and those that fall outside the pale of
acceptability. Because the dominant ideologies defined themselves as reflecting and incarnating reason, both presiding over
action and determining presumptively universal paradigms, to
reject these views was said to be choosing "adventure" over "science" and seemed to imply opting for uncertainty over intellectual and spiritual security. During this period, Western social
science continued to have a strong social position and utilized its
economic advantage and its spiritual preeminence to propagate
its views as exemplary social science. Furthermore, this mission
of Western social science proved enormously attractive to social
scientists in the rest of the world, who saw adopting these views
and practices as joining in a universal community of scholarship.

The challenge to the parochialism of social science since the late 1960's was initially, and perhaps most fundamentally, a challenge to its claim to represent universalism. The critics argued that it was in fact parochial. This critique was made by feminists challenging a masculinist orientation, by the various groups challenging Eurocentrism, and later by multiple other groups raising questions about still other biases that they saw as built into the premises of the social sciences. The form of the arguments tended to be parallel, even if the historical details differed: demonstrations of the reality of the bias, assertions about its consequences in terms of topics of research and subjects studied, accusations concerning the historically narrow social base from which researchers were recruited, and questioning of the epistemological underpinnings of the analyses.

It is important in analyzing these critiques to distinguish the epistemological challenge from the political challenge, even if the two were linked for many persons on both sides of the intellectual debate. The political challenge had to do with the recruitment of personnel (students, professors) within the university structures (going in tandem with a similar challenge in the larger political world). It was alleged that there are all sorts of "forgotten" groups in the social sciences–women, the non-West as a whole, "minority" groups within Western countries, and other groups historically defined as politically and socially marginal.

One of the main arguments made in favor of ending the personnel exclusions in the structures of knowledge was potential implications for the acquisition of valid knowledge. At the most simple level, it was said, most social scientists had studied themselves over the past two centuries, however it was they had de-

fined themselves, and even those studying "others" had tended
to define the others as reflections of or contrasts to themselves.
The solution that was advocated followed quite clearly: if we expanded the scope of recruitment for the scholarly community,
we would probably expand the scope of its objects of study. And
so in fact it proved, as can be seen by a quick comparison of the
titles of papers at current scholarly conferences or the titles of
books being published currently with equivalent lists of the
1950's. In part, this was the natural result of the quantitative expansion of the number of social scientists and the need to find
niches of specialization, but it was also clearly the consequence
of pressures to establish a widened social base in recruiting
scholars and an increased legitimation of new areas of research.

The challenge to parochialism has, however, been deeper
than the question of the social origins of researchers. The new
voices among the social scientists raised theoretical questions
that went beyond the question of the topics or subjects of legitimate study, and even beyond the argument that evaluations are
made differently from different perspectives. The argument of
these new voices was also that there have been presuppositions
built into the theoretical reasoning of the social sciences (and
indeed into that of the natural sciences and the humanities as
well), many of which in fact incorporated *a priori* prejudices or
modes or reasoning that have neither theoretical nor empirical
justification, and that these *a priori* elements ought to be eluci-
dated, analyzed, and replaced by more justifiable premises.

It is in this sense that these demands were part of a demand to
open the social sciences. It does not mean that every new propo-
sition put forth in the name of such new theorizing is correct or

justifiable. It does argue that the enterprise of submitting our theoretical premises to inspection for hidden, unjustified *a priori* assumptions is eminently worthwhile and constitutes in many ways a priority for the social sciences today. These new modes of analysis call for the use of scholarship, analysis, and reasoning to engage in reflection concerning the place and weight in our theorizing of difference (race, gender, sexuality, class).

In 1978, Engelbert Mveng, an African scholar, wrote: "The West agrees with us today that the way to truth passes by numerous paths, other than Aristotelian, Thomistic logic or Hegelian dialectic. But social and human sciences themselves must be decolonized."[8] The call for inclusion, the call for elucidation of theoretical premises has been a call for decolonization, that is, for a transformation of the power relationships which created the particular form of institutionalization of the social sciences that we have known.

The different theories of modernization identified aspects of traditional societies which contrast with those of modern society, but in the process they tended to overlook the complexity of their internal orders. There exist alternative views of such key social science concepts as power and identity. It is possible to detect in a number of non-Western discourses concepts and logics proposing that power is transient and unreal, or that legitimacy must come from the substantive content rather than from the formal procedure. For example, the Mahayana Buddhist applica-

---

8. Engelbert Mveng, "Récents développements de la théologie africaine," *Bulletin of African Theology* 5, no. 9 (1983): 141.

tion of the concept of "maya" to the state, the powerful, and the ruling clans disproves the omnipresence of the logic of power, predominant among the monotheist discourses. The Daoist concept of the legitimate "path" (*dao*) conceives legitimacy as an existential association with the chaotic realities beyond the bureaucratic legitimacy of Confucianism. As for identity, Mahayana Buddhists believe that identity is not absolute and must always be accompanied by an acceptance of the other communities. In the Caribbean (and elsewhere in the Afro-Americas) the boundaries between linguistic, religious, and musical forms on the one hand and ethno-racial categories on the other have been fluid, and individuals have moved across them with some ease. While some Western social scientists have referred pejoratively to the generation of inordinate numbers of cases of multiple identity, local populations have tended to view this as an advantage rather than as an impediment.

The point is not to argue the merits of alternative views of power or identity, but rather to suggest the need for the social sciences to intrude this debate into the very foundations of their analytical constructs. If social science is an exercise in the search for universal knowledge, then the "other" cannot logically exist, for the "other" is part of "us"—the us that is studied, the us that is engaged in studying.

Universalism and particularism are, in short, not necessarily opposed. How do we go beyond this limiting framework? The tensions between universalism and particularism are not a new discovery, but the center of a recurring debate in the social sciences over the last two centuries in many different guises. Universalism has been attacked as being a disguised form of particularism, and as such quite oppressive. Certainly some things are universally true. The problem is that those who hold social power have a natural tendency to see the current situation as universal since it benefits them. The definition of universal truth thereby has changed with changes in the constellation of power.

Scientific truth is itself historical. The issue therefore is not simply what is universal but what is evolving, and whether that which is evolving is necessarily identifiable with progress. How can the social sciences deal with the fact that they must describe, formulate true statements about, an unequal world in which the social scientists themselves are rooted? The claims of universalism have always been claims made by particular persons, and these claimants usually have found themselves in opposition to persons with competing claims. The fact that there are competing particularist views of what is universal forces us to take seriously questions about the neutrality of the scholar. The natural sciences have long accepted the reality that the measurer intrudes on the measured. And yet this statement has remained controversial in the social sciences where, if anything, it might seem more obvious.

Here it may be useful to note that the recent discussion about universalism has blended three questions: the distinction between descriptive and analytic statements (both of which can simultaneously be true); the validity of statements reflecting competing interests (all of which may be equally valid and equally self-interested); and critical rationality as the basis of scholarly communication. We may wish to distinguish what is hidden be-

hind universalism and particularism as categories: as objects, as
objectives, as languages, and as metalanguages. Bringing the
metalanguages to the fore and subjecting them to critical rationality may be the only way in which we can choose our mix
of the universal and the particular as objects, objectives, and
languages.                                                  *– dependents*

If universalism, all universalisms, are historically contingent,
is there any way to construct a relevant single universalism for
the present time? Is the solution to contingent universalism that
of ghettos or that of social integration? Is there a deeper universalism which goes beyond the formalistic universalism of modern societies and modern thought, one that accepts contradictions within its universality? Can we promote a pluralistic universalism, on the analogy of the Indian pantheon, wherein a
single god has many avatars? *incarnations        Vishnu.*

Those with less power are always in some sense in a double
bind: there is no good answer to the prevailing universalisms. If
they accept the wisdom of those universalisms, they find themselves excluded or demeaned by the very premises of the theorizing. But if they hesitate to act with regard to the prevailing universalisms, they find themselves unable to function adequately
within the system, either politically or intellectually, and therefore impede ameliorating the situation. The consequence is
that, initially, those who are excluded move back and forth, both
politically and culturally, between integration and separation.
When this becomes too wearing, they sometimes turn to tearing
down the current universalisms altogether. The social sciences
are currently faced with such attempts. The question before us is
how to open the social sciences so that they may respond ade-

quately and fully to the legitimate objections to parochialism and thereby justify the claim to universal relevance or applicability or validity.

We start from the very strong belief that some kind of universalism is the necessary goal of the community of discourse. At the same time, we recognize that any universalism is historically contingent in that it provides the medium of translation while at the same time setting the terms of the intellectual discussion and is thus a source of intellectual power. We recognize further that every universalism sets off responses to itself, and that these responses are in some sense determined by the nature of the reigning universalism(s). And we believe that it is important to accept the coexistence of different interpretations of an uncertain and complex world. Only a pluralistic universalism will permit us to grasp the richness of the social realities in which we live and have lived.

## 3. The Reality and Validity of the Distinction Between the "Two Cultures"

There have been two striking developments within the structures of knowledge since the 1960's. They come from opposite ends of the university's divisions of knowledge, but both have called into question the reality and the validity of the distinction between the "two cultures." The long-simmering discontents with Newtonian assumptions in the natural sciences, which can be traced at least to Poincaré in the late nineteenth century, began to explode: in intellectual production, in numbers of adherents, in public visibility. This was no doubt in part a result of the same kind of pressure for differentiation from sheer numerical growth which was playing its role in the turmoil of the social sciences. But, more importantly, it was the outcome of the increasing inability of the older scientific theories to offer plausible solutions to the difficulties encountered as scientists sought to solve problems concerning ever more complex phenomena.

These developments in the natural sciences and mathematics were important for the social sciences in two ways. First, the model of nomothetic epistemology, which had become ever more dominant in the social sciences in the post-1945 period, was based precisely on applying the wisdom of Newtonian concepts to the study of social phenomena. The rug was being pulled out from under the use of this model in the social sciences. Second, new developments in the natural sciences emphasized nonlinearity over linearity, complexity over simplification, the impossibility of removing the measurer from the measurement, and even, for some mathematicians, the superiority of qualitative interpretative scope over a quantitative precision that is more limited in accuracy. Most important of all, these scientists emphasized the arrow of time. In short, the natural sciences were beginning to seem closer to what had been scorned as "soft" social science than to what had been touted as "hard" social science. This not only began to change the power balance in the internal struggles in the social sciences, but also served to reduce the strong distinction between natural science and social science as "superdomains." This lessening of the contradictions between the natural sciences and the social sciences did not now imply, however, as in previous attempts, conceiving of humanity as mechanical, but rather instead conceiving of nature as active and creative.

The Cartesian view of classical science had described the world as an automaton, which was deterministic and capable of total description in the form of causal laws, or "laws of nature." Today many natural scientists would argue that the world should be described quite differently.[9] It is a more unstable world, a much more complex world, a world in which perturbations play a big role, one of whose key questions is how to explain how such complexity arises. Most natural scientists no longer believe that the macroscopic can simply be deduced in principle from a simpler microscopic world. Many now believe that complex systems are self-organizing, and that consequently nature can no longer be considered to be passive.

It is not that they believe Newtonian physics to be wrong, but that the stable, time-reversible systems which Newtonian science described represent only a special, limited segment of reality. Newtonian physics describes, for example, the motion of the planets but not the development of the planetary system. It describes systems at equilibrium or near to equilibrium but not systems far from equilibrium, conditions that are at least as frequent, if not more frequent, than systems at equilibrium. The conditions of a system far from equilibrium are not time-reversible, in which it is sufficient to know the "law" and the initial conditions in order to predict its future states. Rather, a system far from equilibrium is the expression of an "arrow of time," whose role is essential and constructive. In such a system, the future is uncertain and the conditions are irreversible. The laws that we can formulate therefore enumerate only possibilities, never certainties.

---

9. See Ilya Prigogine, *Les lois du chaos* (Paris: Flammarion, 1994).

Consequently, irreversibility is no longer considered to be a scientific misperception, the outcome of approximations resulting from the inadequacy of scientific knowledge. Rather, natural scientists today are working to extend the formulation of the laws of dynamics to include irreversibility and probability. Only in this way, it is now thought, may scientists hope to understand the mechanisms which, at the fundamental level of description, drive the restless universe in which we are embedded. Natural science is hoping thereby to make the idea of laws of nature compatible with the idea of events, of novelty, and of creativity. In a sense, it could be argued that instability plays a role for physical phenomena analogous to that of Darwin's natural selection in biology. Natural selection is a necessary but not sufficient condition for evolution. Some species have appeared only recently; others have persisted for hundreds of millions of years. Similarly, the existence of probabilities and the breaking of time symmetry is a necessary condition of evolution.

The importance of complex systems analysis for the analysis of social science is far-reaching. Historical social systems are quite clearly composed of multiple, interacting units, characterized by the emergence and evolution of nested hierarchical organization and structure, and complex spatiotemporal behavior. Furthermore, in addition to the kind of complexity exhibited by nonlinear dynamic systems with fixed, microscopic mechanisms of interaction, historical social systems are composed of individual elements capable of internal adaptation and learning as a result of their experience. This adds a new level of complexity (one which is shared with evolutionary biology and ecology) beyond that of the nonlinear dynamics of traditional physical systems.

The methods of complex systems analysis have already been applied in various areas, such as the problem of the relationship between stochastically generated innovations and long-term economic fluctuations, which seem to display the characteristics of deterministic chaos. Furthermore, it can be shown how competing technologies, in the presence of increasing returns of various sorts, may become "locked in," despite the availability of superior alternatives. The conceptual framework offered by evolutionary complex systems as developed by the natural sciences presents to the social sciences a coherent set of ideas that matches long-standing views in the social sciences, particularly among those who have been resistant to the forms of nomothetic analysis inspired by the science of linear equilibria. Scientific analysis based on the dynamics of nonequilibria, with its emphasis on multiple futures, bifurcation and choice, historical dependence, and, for some, intrinsic and inherent uncertainty resonates well with important traditions of the social sciences.

The second great challenge to the tripartite division of knowledge into three great domains emerged out of the "humanistic" end of the tension between the two cultures. This challenge came from what we may generically call "cultural studies." "Culture," of course, was a term that had long been used both by anthropologists and by scholars in the humanities, but not usually with this new, rather more political, thrust. The study of culture as a quasi-discipline exploded, with its programs, its journals, its associations, and its library collections. There seem to be three main themes involved in this challenge. None of these themes is new. What is perhaps new is that they have become associated with one another, and collectively have shown strength such that these views are having a major influence in the institutional arenas of knowledge production for the first time in the two centuries since science, a certain science, displaced philosophy, a certain philosophy, from the position of legitimator of knowledge.

The three themes that have come together in cultural studies are: first, the central importance of gender studies and all kinds of "non-Eurocentric" studies to the study of historical social systems; second, the importance of local, very situated historical analysis, associated by many with a new "hermeneutic turn"; third, the assessment of the values involved in technological achievements in relation to other values. While the study of culture attracted people in almost all the disciplines, it was particularly popular among three groups: among scholars in literary studies of all kinds, for whom it legitimated a concern with the current social and political scene; among anthropologists, for some of whom the new emphases offered a domain to replace (or at least compete with) that of ethnography, which had lost its commanding role within the discipline; and among persons involved in the new quasi-disciplines relating to the "forgotten" peoples of modernity (those neglected by virtue of gender, race, class, etc.), for whom it provided a theoretical ("postmodern") framework for their elaborations of difference.

We have already discussed the attempts to overcome the parochial heritage of the social sciences. What does it add to consider this within the framework of questioning the validity of the distinction between the two cultures? In the framing of the issue of the two cultures, there had always been an unexpressed but quite real assumption. It had been implied that science was more ra-

tional, "harder" and more precise, more powerful, more serious, more efficacious, and therefore more consequential than
philosophy or arts and letters. The latent premise was that it was
somehow more modern, more European, and more masculine.
It is to these unspoken assertions that the proponents of gender
studies and of all the non-Eurocentric studies have been react-
ing in putting forward their views and their demands within the
framework of a revalorization of cultural studies.

Basically, the same issue emerged in the question sometimes
framed as the local versus the universal, sometimes framed as
agency versus structure. Structures / the universal were asserted
to be impersonal, eternal or at least very long-lasting, and beyond control by human effort–but not quite beyond everyone's
control: structures seemed manipulable by rational, scientific
experts, but not by ordinary people, and not by groups that were
less powerful within the structures. Asserting the continuing ef-
fectiveness of structures in the analysis of social phenomena was
said to imply the irrelevance of social mobilization and therefore
of attempts by the less powerful to transform the social situation.
The universal was said to be remote, whereas the "local" was
deemed immediate. In local arenas, the centrality of gender and
race/ethnicity to analysis seemed self-evidently relevant. The
more worldwide the arena, the more difficult it was thought to
organize effectively to present alternative perspectives, defend
alternative interests, assert alternative epistemologies.

The third element in the affirmation of cultural studies has
been the expression of skepticism concerning the merits of technological advance. The degree of skepticism has ranged from
moderate doubts to extreme rejections of the products of this

technology. It has taken political form in a wide array of ecological concerns and movements, and intellectual form in the return of values to center stage in scholarly analysis (what some might phrase as the return of philosophy). Faced with the ecological crisis, the claims of technology to be universal were put into question. Postmodern skepticism was replacing modern criticism, and almost all so-called grand theories came under attack in the name of a highly abstract mode of theorizing. The culturalist impact made itself felt across the disciplines. Hermeneutic approaches regained ground they had lost before. In different disciplines, language became a central locus of discussion, both as an object of study and as a key to the discipline's epistemological self-reflection.

Cultural studies has offered solutions for some existing problems, but it has also created others. The stress on agency and meaning has sometimes led to a quasi-voluntaristic neglect of real structural constraints on human behavior. Emphasizing the importance of local spaces can lead to a neglect of the broader interrelations of the historical fabric. Postmodernist skepticism has sometimes led to a sweeping antitheoretical stance that condemned other perspectives that were equally critical of the limitations of a positivist approach. We continue to believe that the search for coherence is a continuing obligation of a reconstructed historical social science.

Still, the rise of cultural studies had an impact on the social sciences in some ways analogous to the new developments in science. Just as the new arguments of the natural scientists undermined the organizational divide between the superdomains of the natural and the social sciences, so the arguments of the advocates of cultural studies undermined the organizational divide between the superdomains of the social sciences and the humanities. These culturalist projects have challenged all existing theoretical paradigms, even those that were themselves critical of mainstream nomothetic social science. The support for such views was to be found across the various disciplines of the humanities and the social sciences, and this brought about forms of intellectual cooperation that have ignored the traditional line between the humanities and the social sciences.

Before 1945, the social sciences were internally split between the two cultures, and there were many voices who urged the social sciences to disappear by merging either into the natural sciences or into the humanities, according to one's preferences. In a sense, the social sciences were being called upon to accept the deep reality of the concept of two cultures and to enter the one or the other *on its terms*. Today, the discovery of common themes and approaches seems to be occurring on different bases than in the past. Natural scientists are talking of the arrow of time, which is what has always been central to the more humanistic wing of the social sciences. At the same time, literary scholars are talking of "theory." However hermeneutic such theorizing is and however hostile it proclaims itself to master narratives, theorizing is not what literary scholars used to do. No doubt, this is not the kind of theory that has always been central to work of the more scientistic wing of the social sciences. Nonetheless for a group to whom the use of terms is so important, it is at least to be noted that the proponents of cultural studies have turned "theory" into one of their code words.

We cannot speak of a real rapprochement between the multiple expressions of the two (or three) cultures. But the debates have aroused doubts about the clarity of the distinctions. And we seem to be moving in the direction of a more noncontradictory view of the multiple domains of knowledge. In a strange way, the shifts in viewpoint in all fields seem to be moving more toward than away from the traditional standpoints of the social sciences. May we then say that the concept of two cultures is in the process of being overcome? It is much too early to tell. What is clear is that the tripartite division between the natural sciences, the social sciences, and the humanities is no longer as self-evident as it once seemed. It also now seems that the social sciences are no longer a poor relative somehow torn between the two polarized clans of the natural sciences and the humanities; rather they have become the locus of their potential reconciliation.

# III. What Kind of Social Science Shall We Now Build?

> In any social circumstance, there are only a limited
> number of ways in which a clash of values can be dealt
> with. One is through geographical segregation. . . .
> Another, more active way, is through exit. . . . A third way
> of coping with individual or cultural difference is through
> dialogue. Here a clash of values can in principle operate
> under a positive sign—it can be a means of increased
> communication and self-understanding. . . . Finally,
> a clash of values can be resolved through the use of
> force or violence. . . . In the globalizing society in which
> we now live the first two of these four options become
> drastically reduced.
>
> —Anthony Giddens [10]

What are the implications of the multiple debates
within the social sciences since 1945 for the kind of social science
we now should build? And for what, exactly, are they implications? The intellectual implications of these debates are not entirely consonant with the organizational structure of the social
sciences that we have inherited. Thus, as we begin to resolve the
intellectual debates, we must decide what to do organizationally.
It may turn out to be easier to do the former than the latter.

The most immediate question is the organizational structure
of the social sciences themselves. They have, of course, been disciplines, which meant that they were intended to shape the
training of future scholars, and this they have done effectively.

10. Anthony Giddens, *Beyond Left and Right* (Stanford: Stanford
University Press, 1995), p. 19.

But in the final analysis, training of students has not been the most powerful mechanism of control. A stronger one was the fact that the disciplines have controlled the career patterns of scholars once they completed their training. Both teaching and research positions in universities and research structures have by and large required a doctorate (or its equivalent), and for most positions the doctorate has had to be in a specified discipline. Publication in the official and quasi-official journals of the discipline to which one is organizationally attached was, and for the most part still is, considered a necessary step for career advancement. Graduate students are still advised (and well advised) to secure their degrees in a discipline that is considered a standard one. Scholars have tended to attend primarily the national (and international) meetings of their own discipline. Disciplinary structures have covered their members with a protective screen, and have been wary of encouraging crossing the lines.

Yet disciplinary prerequisites have been breaking down in some scholarly arenas that have become important since 1945. The worldwide series of colloquia and conferences, so central in recent decades to scientific communication, have tended to recruit participants according to specific subject matter, for the most part without too much regard for disciplinary affiliations. There are today a growing number of major scientific reviews that consciously ignore the disciplinary boundaries. And of course the multiple new quasi-disciplines and/or "programs" which have been emerging in the last half century are often, even usually, composed of persons who have degrees from multiple disciplines.

Most importantly, there is the eternal battle for resource allocation, which in recent years has gotten more ferocious because of budgetary constraints, after a long period of continuous budgetary expansion. As newly emerging quasi-disciplinary structures lay greater claims on university resources and seek to control more directly future appointments, they tend to eat into the power of the existing main disciplines. In this battle, groups which are presently less well financed seek to define abstract intellectual justifications for proposed shifts in resource allocation. It is here that the main organizational pressure for restructuring of the social sciences will come. The problem is that this pressure to realign organizational structures on the basis of new intellectual categories is pursued country by country, university by university. And the initiative is often not that of working scholars but that of administrators, whose concerns are sometimes more budgetary than intellectual. The perspective before us is that of organizational dispersal, with a multiplicity of names, akin to the situation that existed in the first half of the nineteenth century. That is to say, the process of establishing the disciplines between, say, 1850 and 1945 was one of reducing the number of categories into which social science might be divided into a limited list with which we have become familiar and which was largely adopted worldwide. We have recounted how and why the process since then has begun to move in the other direction. We may wish to reflect on the rationality of the emerging pattern.

These organizational problems are, of course, more than compounded by the blurring of the trimodal pattern of superdomains: the natural sciences, the social sciences, and the humanities. It thus becomes a question not merely of the possible reconfiguration of organizational boundaries within the social science disciplines, but of the possible reconfiguration of the larger structures of the so-called faculties. Of course, this struggle over boundaries has been a ceaseless one. But there come moments in which what may be called for are major as opposed to minor realignments. The early nineteenth century ushered in such a pattern of major realignments, which we have been describing here. The question before us is whether the early twenty-first century may be another such moment.

There is a third level of possible restructuring. It is not only a question of the boundaries of departments within the faculties and the boundaries of faculties within the universities. Part of the nineteenth-century restructuring involved the revival of the university itself as the central locus of knowledge creation and reproduction. The enormous expansion of the university system across the world in the period since 1945, in terms of numbers of institutions, of teaching personnel, and of students, has led to a flight of research activities to ever "higher" levels of the educational system. Before 1945, some researchers still taught in secondary schools. By 1990, not only was this no longer true, but many scholars even avoided, to the degree they could, teaching in the first or lower levels of the university system. Today, some are even fleeing the teaching of doctoral students. As a result, there has been a growth of "institutes of advanced studies" and other nonteaching structures.

Similarly, the central locus of intellectual communication in the nineteenth century was national scholarly meetings and national scientific journals. As these structures became overcrowded, they were to some extent replaced by colloquia, which have flourished worldwide since 1945. Now this field too is over-crowded, and we are seeing the emergence of small, continuing structures of physically separated scholars, abetted, of course, by the great advances in communications possibilities offered by electronic networks. All these developments at least open the question of whether, in the next fifty years, universities as such will continue to be the main organizational base of scholarly research. Or are other structures–independent research institutes, centers for advanced study, networks, epistemic communities via electronic facilities–going to substitute for them in a significant way? These developments may represent very positive adjustments to the problems inherent in the enormous expansion of university structures. But if it is thought desirable or inevitable that research become separated to any significant extent from teaching and from the university system, there will need to be a greater effort to obtain public legitimation for this development, or else there may not be the material bases to sustain scholarly research.

These organizational problems, which are of course not limited to the social sciences, frame the context within which intellectual clarification will take place. There are probably three central theoretical/methodological issues around which it is necessary to construct new, heuristic consensuses in order to permit fruitful advances in knowledge. The first concerns the relationship of the researcher to the research. At the beginning of the century, Max Weber summarized the trajectory of modern thought as the "disenchantment of the world." To be sure, his phrase merely described a process that had evolved over several hundred years. In *La nouvelle alliance*, Ilya Prigogine and

Isabelle Stengers have called for a "reenchantment of the world." The concept of the "disenchantment of the world" represented the search for an objective knowledge unconstrained by revealed and/or accepted wisdom or ideology. In the social sciences, it was a demand that we not rewrite history in the name of existing power structures. This demand was an essential step in freeing intellectual activity from disabling external pressures and from mythology, and remains valid. We have no wish to return the pendulum and find ourselves once again in the predicament out of which the disenchantment of the world sought to rescue us.

The call for a "reenchantment of the world" is a different one. It is not a call for mystification. It is a call to break down the artificial boundaries between humans and nature, to recognize that they both form part of a single universe framed by the arrow of time. The reenchantment of the world is meant to liberate human thought still further. The problem has been that, in the attempt to liberate the human spirit, the concept of the neutral scientist (put forward not by Weber but by positivist social science) offered an impossible solution to the laudable objective of freeing scholarship from arbitrary orthodoxy. No scientist can ever be extracted from his/her physical and social context. Every measurement changes reality in the attempt to record it. Every conceptualization is based on philosophical commitments. In time, the widespread belief in a fictive neutrality has become itself a major obstacle to increasing the truth value of our findings. If this poses a great problem for the natural scientists, it is an even greater problem for the social scientists. Translating the reenchantment of the world into a reasonable working practice will not be easy. But for social scientists it seems an urgent task.

The second issue is how to reinsert time and space as internal variables constitutive of our analyses and not merely unchanging physical realities within which the social universe exists. If we consider that concepts of time and space are socially constructed variables which the world (and the scholar) use to affect and interpret social reality, we are faced with the necessity of developing a methodology wherein we shall place these social constructions at the center of our analyses, but in ways that they will not be seen or used as arbitrary phenomena. To the extent that we succeed in this, the outdated distinction between idiographic and nomothetic epistemologies will lose whatever cognitive meaning it still has. However, this is easier said than done.

The third issue before us is how to overcome the artificial separations erected in the nineteenth century between supposedly autonomous realms of the political, the economic, and the social (or the cultural or the sociocultural). In the current practice of social scientists, the lines are de facto often ignored. But the current practice does not accord with the official viewpoints of the major disciplines. The question of the existence of these separate realms needs to be tackled directly, or rather, to be reopened quite fully. Once that happens, and new formulations begin to take root, the intellectual bases for the restructuring of the disciplines may become clearer.

One last caution. If the researcher cannot be "neutral" and time and space are internal variables in the analysis, then it follows that the task of restructuring the social sciences must be one that results from the interaction of scholars coming from every clime and perspective (and taking into account gender, race, class, and linguistic culture), and that this worldwide interaction be a real one and not a mere formal courtesy masking the imposition of the views of one segment of world scientists. It will not be at all easy to organize such worldwide interaction in a meaningful way. It is thus a further obstacle in our path. However, overcoming this obstacle may be the key to overcoming all the others.

What, therefore, can we conclude about the possible steps that could be taken in order to "open social science"? There exists no easily available blueprint on the basis of which we can decree any reorganization of the structures of knowledge. We are concerned rather with encouraging collective discussion and making some suggestions about paths along which solutions might be found. Before we consider proposals for restructuring, there seem to us several major dimensions worthy of fuller debate and analysis. They are: (1) the implications of refusing the ontological distinction between humans and nature, a distinction embedded in modern thought since at least Descartes; (2) the implications of refusing to consider the state as providing the only possible and/or primary boundaries within which social action occurs and is to be analyzed; (3) the implications of accepting the unending tension between the one and the many, the universal and the particular, as a permanent feature of human society and not as an anachronism; (4) the kind of objectivity which is plausible in the light of the evolving premises of science.

## 1. Humans and Nature

The social sciences have been moving in the direction of an increasing respect for nature at the same time that the natural sciences have been moving in the direction of seeing the universe as unstable and unpredictable, thereby conceiving of the universe as an active reality and not an automaton subject to domination by humans, who are somehow located outside nature. The convergences between the natural and social sciences become greater to the degree one views both as dealing with complex systems, in which future developments are the outcome of temporally irreversible processes.

Some social scientists have responded to recent findings in behavioral genetics by urging a more biological orientation for the social sciences. Some have even been reviving the ideas of genetic determinism on the basis of inferences from the human genome project. We think that taking this path would be a serious mistake and a setback for the social sciences. We feel that the principal lesson of recent developments in the natural sciences is rather that the complexity of social dynamics needs to be taken more seriously than ever.

Utopias are part of the concern of the social sciences, which is not true of the natural sciences, and utopias must of course be based on existing trends. Although we now are clear that there is no future certainty, and cannot be one, nonetheless images of the future influence how humans act in the present. The university cannot remain aloof in a world in which, since certainty is excluded, the role of the intellectual is necessarily changing and the idea of the neutral scientist is under severe challenge, as we have documented. Concepts of utopias are related to ideas of possible progress, but their realization does not depend merely on the advance of the natural sciences, as many previously thought, but rather on the increase in human creativity, the expression of the self in this complex world.

We come from a social past of conflicting certitudes, be they related to science, ethics, or social systems, to a present of considerable questioning, including questioning about the intrinsic possibility of certainties. Perhaps we are witnessing the end of a type of rationality that is no longer appropriate to our time. The accent we call for is one placed on the complex, the temporal, and the unstable, which corresponds today to a transdisciplinary movement gaining in vigor. This is by no means a call to abandon the concept of substantive rationality. As Whitehead said so well, the project which remains central both to the students of human social life and to the natural scientists is the intelligibility of the world: "to frame a coherent, logical, necessary system of general ideas in terms of which every element of our experience can be interpreted." [11]

In the choice of possible futures, resources are very much a political question, and the demand for expanded participation in decision making is worldwide. We call upon the social sciences to open themselves to these questions. This is by no means a call, however, as was made in the nineteenth century, for a social physics. Rather, it is a recognition that, though the explanations we may make of the historical structuring of the natural universe and of human experience are by no means identical,

11. A. N. Whitehead, *Process and Reality*, corrected ed. (New York: Macmillan, 1978), p. 3.

they are noncontradictory and are both related to evolution. During the past two centuries, the real world has imposed current political issues on intellectual activity, pressuring scholars to define particular phenomena as universals because of their implications in the immediate political situation. The issue is how to escape the passing constraints of the contemporary to arrive at more long-term, durable, and useful interpretations of social reality. In the necessary differentiation and specialization of the social sciences, we may have paid too little attention to one general social problem resulting from the creation of knowledge: how not to create a gap between those who know and those who do not.

The responsibility of going beyond these immediate pressures is not that of the working social scientists alone; it also is that of intellectual bureaucracies–university administrators, scholarly associations, foundations, government agencies responsible for education and research. It requires the recognition that the major issues facing a complex society cannot be solved by decomposing them into small parts that seem easy to manage analytically, but rather by attempting to treat these problems, treat humans and nature, in their complexity and interrelations.

## 2. The State as an Analytic Building Block

The social sciences have been very state-centric in the sense that states formed the supposedly self-evident frameworks within which the processes analyzed by the social sciences took place. This was especially true for those that studied (at least up to 1945) essentially the Western world–history and the trio of nomothetic social sciences (economics, political science, and sociology). To be sure, neither anthropology nor Oriental studies was state-centric, but this was because the zones these scholars studied were not considered to be loci of modern social structures. Modern social structures were implicitly located within modern states. After 1945, with the rise of area studies and the consequent expansion of the empirical domain of history and the three nomothetic social sciences into the non-Western world, these non-Western areas too became subject to state-centric analyses. The key post-1945 concept of "development" referred first and foremost to the development of each state, taken as an individual entity.

No doubt there were always some social scientists who did not consider the state–the current state, the historical state (pushed backward into prestate times), the putative state–to be a unit so natural that its analytic primacy was presumed, not justified. But these dissenters were few and not all that vocal in the period from 1850 to 1950. The self-evident character of the state as constituting the natural boundary of social life began to be questioned much more seriously beginning in the 1970's. This was the result of the conjuncture, a not accidental conjuncture, of two transformations. The first was a transformation in the real world. The states seemed to lose their promise as agents of modernization and economic well-being in popular and scholarly esteem. And second, there were the changes in the world of knowledge we have been describing, which led scholars to look again at previously unquestioned presuppositions.

The certain knowledge that had been promised us by social scientists seemed an evident consequence of their faith in progress. It found expression in the belief in steady improvements that would be implemented by "experts," in which the "enabling" state would play a key role in the effort to reform society. The social sciences were expected to abet this process of rational, gradual improvement. It seemed to follow that the state's boundaries would be taken as forming the natural cadre within which to pursue such improvement. There have been, of course, continual challenges within the world of knowledge, including within the social sciences (for example, in the late nineteenth century), to an overly simple idea of progress. But each previous challenge seemed to melt away in the face of continuing technological achievements. Furthermore, the basic thrust of democratization led everywhere to steadily increasing demands on the state, urgent calls for it to utilize its fiscal and budgetary powers to ameliorate and redistribute. The state as purveyor of progress thus seemed theoretically secure.

But in recent decades, as redistributions increased less fast than escalating demands for redistribution, states began to be viewed as offering less satisfaction rather than more. A certain amount of disillusionment began to set in, beginning in the 1960's. Insofar as the transformations of the world since then have served to nourish a deep skepticism in most parts of the world about how really inevitable the promised improvement might be, and in particular whether the state's reforms in fact bring about real improvements, the naturalness of the state as the unit of analysis has been seriously undermined. "Think globally; act locally" is a slogan that very deliberately leaves out the state, and represents a withdrawal of faith in the state as a mechanism of reform. It would have been impossible in the

1950's, when both ordinary people and scholars thought at the state level and acted at the state level.

Given this shift from action at the state level, which was thought to guarantee a certain future, to action at global and local levels, which appears much more uncertain and difficult to manipulate, the new modes of analysis of both the natural scientists and of the proponents of cultural studies seemed to many to offer more plausible models. Both modes of analysis took uncertainties (and localisms) to be central analytic variables, not to be buried in a deterministic universalism. It followed that the self-evident nature of states as conceptual containers—the analytic derivative in the social sciences of both idiographic history and the more universalistic social sciences—became open to serious challenge and to debate.

State-centric thinking had not, of course, precluded the study of relations between states, international relations as it is commonly (if erroneously) called, and subfields existed within each of the social sciences devoted to the so-called international arena. We might have expected that it would be practitioners from within these subfields who would first respond to the challenge that the rising awareness of trans-state phenomena has presented to the analytic frameworks of the social sciences, but this was not in fact the case. The problem was that international studies had been premised on a state-centric framework just as much as other parts of the social sciences. They took the form primarily of comparative studies, with states as the unit to be compared, or of "foreign policy" studies, in which the object was to study the policies of states towards each other, rather than that of studying the emergent characteristics of trans-state structures. In the institutionalized social sciences, the study of the complex structures that exist at the more global level were for a long time largely neglected, just as were the complex structures that exist at more local levels.

Since the late 1960's, there have been numerous attempts—within each of the disciplines and across the disciplines—to be less state-centric. In most cases this has gone in tandem with historicization and, in particular, with the use of longer time periods for empirical analysis. This shift in the unit of analysis has gone under many labels, such as international political economy, the study of world cities, a global institutional economics, world history, world-systems analysis, and civilizational studies. There has simultaneously been a renewed concern with "regions"—both regions that are large and trans-state (e.g., the recent concern with East Asia as a region within the whole world) and regions that are small and located inside states (e.g., the proto-industrialization concept in economic history). This is not the place to review each of these in their commonalities and their differences, but to note that each in its way challenged the state-centric theoretical presuppositions of the social sciences as they had been traditionally institutionalized. It remains to be seen how far the logic of their positions will push their proponents. There are some who favor a clean break with the traditional disciplines rather than remaining on their fringe, wishing to join a new heterodoxy based upon global spatial referents.

The state-centrism of traditional social science analyses was a theoretical simplification that involved the presumption of homogeneous and equivalent spaces, each of which formed an autonomous system operating largely through parallel processes. The limits of this kind of simplification ought to be even more evident in the study of complex historical social systems than they were in the study of atomic and molecular phenomena, in which such methods are now considered a thing of the past.

Of course, rejection of the state as the indicated socio-geographical container for social analysis in no way means that the state is no longer to be viewed as a key institution in the modern world, one that has profound influences on economic, cultural, and social processes. The study of all these processes clearly require an understanding of the mechanisms of the state. What they do not require is the assumption that the state is the natural, or even the most important, boundary of social action. By challenging the efficacy of organizing social knowledge among units defined by state boundaries, recent developments in the social sciences imply some significant transitions in the objects of social scientific research. Once we drop the state-centric assumption, which has been fundamental to history and the nomothetic social sciences in the past, and accept that this perspective can often be a hindrance to making the world intelligible, we inevitably raise questions about the very structure of the disciplinary partitions which have grown up around, indeed have been based on, this assumption.

## 3. The Universal and the Particular

The tension between the universal and the particular in the social sciences has always been a subject of passionate debate, since it has always been seen as having immediate political implications, and this has impinged on serene discussion. The

Romantic reaction to, and reformulation of, Enlightenment conceptions was centered around this issue, and that debate was not unconnected with the political controversies of the Napoleonic era as the culmination of processes launched by the French Revolution. The issue has returned to the fore in contemporary discussions of the social sciences, in large part resulting from the political reassertion of the non-Western world, combined with the parallel political assertion of groups within the Western world that consider themselves to have been culturally oppressed. We have already traced the various forms in which this debate has taken form within the social sciences. One significant organizational consequence of this revived debate has been the call for a social science that is more "multicultural" or intercultural.

The effort to insert new premises into the theoretical frameworks of the social sciences, ones that respond to this demand for a more multicultural social science, has been met with a revival under various guises of social Darwinism. Social Darwinism is a particular variant, and a rather influential one, of the doctrine of inevitable progress. Its key argument has been essentially that progress is the result of a social struggle, in which competency wins out, and that interfering with this social struggle is interfering with social progress. These arguments have sometimes been reinforced by the genetic determinism we have mentioned. The discourse of social Darwinism labels any concept associated with the losers in the "survival of the fittest" evolutionary process as irrational and/or unrealistic. This categorical condemnation has often covered all values held by groups who do not have powerful social positions, as well as alternative projects critical of the belief that industrialization, modernization, and Westernization are inevitably linked.

Technocratic rationality, presenting itself as the most advanced version of modern rationalism, has been in many ways an avatar of social Darwinism. It also delegitimizes any concept which does not fit a means-end model of rationality, and any institution which has no immediate functional utility. The framework that situates individuals primarily within states has tended to treat actors who do not fit in this framework as remnants of premodern times, who will be eliminated eventually by the advance of progress. Treating seriously the innumerable concepts, values, beliefs, norms, and institutions placed in this unwanted category has been deemed unscientific. In many cases, the very existence of these alternative worldviews and their proponents has been forgotten, suppressed from the collective memory of modern societies.

What has changed today is that many people, including many scholars, now strongly refuse to accept this dismissal of alternative sets of values, and this has been reinforced by the (re)discovery of major substantive irrationalities that are embedded in modern rational thought. The question that is consequently before us is how to take seriously in our social science a plurality of worldviews without losing the sense that there exists the possibility of knowing and realizing sets of values that may in fact be common, or become common, to all humanity. The key task is to explode the hermetic language used to describe persons and groups that are "others," who are merely objects of social science analysis, as opposed to those who are subjects having full rights and legitimacy, among whom the analysts have placed

themselves. There is an inevitable confusion or overlap here between the ideological and the epistemological. For a large number of non-Western social scientists, the distinction between the
political, the religious, and the scientific does not seem entirely
reasonable or valid.

Many of the critics of parochialism have hitherto emphasized
the negative agenda, that of denying false universalisms. They
have questioned the appropriateness of claimed universalist
principles to a number of singular cases, and/or the possibility
or desirability of universalism, and have offered in its place
quasi-disciplinary categories defined by social constituencies.
The principal result up to now has been largely the multiplication of particularisms. Beyond the obvious argument that the
voices of dominated (and therefore hitherto largely ignored)
groups need to be acknowledged, there is the more arduous task
of demonstrating how incorporating the experiences of these
groups is fundamental to achieving objective knowledge of social processes.

We would emphasize that universalism is always historically
contingent. Thus, rather than show once again what the social
sciences have missed by excluding a large part of human experience, we should move on to demonstrate what our understanding of social processes gains once we include increasingly larger
segments of the world's historical experiences. Nonetheless,
however parochial the previous versions of universalism have
been, it does not seem sensible simply to abandon the terrain of
the traditional disciplines to those who persist in these paro-
chialisms. Restoring the balance will involve arguing the case
within the existing disciplines, while simultaneously establish-

ing new avenues for dialogue and exchange beyond (and not merely between) the existing disciplines.

We further strongly urge the fuller realization of a multilingual scholarship. The choice of language often predetermines the outcome. To take a very obvious example, the concepts of the middle class, the *bourgeoisie*, and *Bürgertum* (presumably approximately similar) in fact define significantly different categories and imply different empirical measurements. The minimum that we can expect of social scientists is an awareness of the range of realms of conceptual meaning. A world in which all social scientists had working control of several major scholarly languages would be a world in which better social science was done. Knowledge of languages opens the mind of the scholar to other ways of organizing knowledge. It might go a considerable distance towards creating a working and fruitful understanding of the unending tensions of the antinomy of universalism and particularism. But multilingualism will only thrive if it becomes organizationally as well as intellectually legitimated: through the real use of multiple languages in pedagogy; through the real use of multiple languages in scientific meetings.

Dialogue and exchange can only exist where there is basic respect among colleagues. The angry rhetoric that now intrudes on these discussions is, however, a reflection of underlying social tensions. Merely calling for civil debate will not achieve it. Responding simultaneously to the demands of universal relevance (applicability, validity) and of the continuing reality of a multiplicity of cultures will depend on the imaginativeness of our organizational responses and a certain tolerance for intellectual experimentation in the social sciences. The social sciences should embrace a very wide opening to research and teaching on all cultures (societies, peoples) in the search for a renewed, expanded, and meaningful pluralistic universalism.

## 4. Objectivity

The question of objectivity has been central to the methodological debates of the social sciences from the beginning. We said at the outset of this report that social science was the attempt in the modern world "to develop systematic, secular knowledge about reality that is somehow validated empirically." The term "objectivity" has been used to represent appropriate attempts to achieve this objective. The meaning of objectivity has been very much tied to the sense that knowledge is not *a priori*, that research can teach us things that we did not know, can offer surprises vis-à-vis our prior expectations.

The opposite of "objective" was taken to be "subjective," defined most often as the intrusion of the biases of the researcher into the collection and interpretation of the data. This was seen as distorting the data, and therefore of reducing its validity. How then could one be objective? In practice, different social sciences took different paths in the search for this objective. Two models were dominant. The more nomothetic social sciences emphasized removing the danger of subjectivity by maximizing the "hardness" of the data, that is, their measurability and comparability. This pushed them in the direction of collecting data about the present moment, where the researcher was most likely to be able to control the quality of the data. The more idiographic historians analyzed the issue differently. They argued in favor of primary sources, untouched (undistorted) by intermediate persons (previous scholars) and in favor of data about which the researcher would be expected to feel more uninvolved personally. This pushed them in the direction of data created in the past, and therefore about the past, and in the direction of qualitative data, where the richness of the context could lead the researcher to understand the fullness of the motivations involved, as opposed to a situation where the researcher simply extrapolated his own model, seen as his own prejudices, onto the data.

There have always been doubts expressed about the degree to which either of these approaches allows us to obtain objective data. In recent decades, these doubts have been expressed quite loudly, the result of the changing situation in the social sciences that we have been describing. One kind of question that has been posed is "*whose* objectivity?" Posing the question in this way implies skepticism, even total doubt, about the possibility of achieving objective knowledge. Some have suggested that what is said to be objective knowledge is merely the knowledge of those who are socially and politically stronger.

We agree that all scholars are rooted in a specific social setting, and therefore inevitably utilize presuppositions and prejudices that interfere with their perceptions and interpretations of social reality. In this sense, there can be no "neutral" scholar. We also agree that a quasi-photographic representation of social reality is impossible. All data are selections from reality, based on the worldviews or theoretical models of the era, as filtered through the standpoints of particular groups in each era. In this sense, the bases of selection are historically constructed, and will always inevitably change as the world changes. If perfectly uninvolved scholars reproducing a social world outside themselves is what we mean by objectivity, then we do not think such a phenomenon exists.

But there is another meaning to objectivity. Objectivity can be seen as the outcome of human learning, which represents the intent of scholarship and the evidence that it is possible. Scholars seek to convince each other of the validity of their findings and their interpretations. They appeal to the fact that they have used methods that are replicable by others, methods whose details they present openly to others. They appeal to the coherence and utility of their interpretations in explaining the largest amount of available data, larger amounts than alternative explanations. In short, they present themselves to the intersubjective judgment of all those who do research or think systematically about the particular subject.

We accept that this objective has not been realized fully, or even frequently, up to now. We accept that there have been systematic errors in the ways in which social scientists have proceeded in the past, and that many have used the mask of objectivity to pursue their subjective views. We have indeed tried to outline the nature of such continuing distortions. And we accept that these errors are not to be repaired by simple appeals to an ideal of intersubjectivity, but require strengthening the organizational underpinnings of the collective effort. What we do not accept is that social science is therefore to be reduced to a miscellany of private views, each equally valid.

We feel that pushing the social sciences in the direction of combatting the fragmentation of knowledge is also pushing it in the direction of a meaningful degree of objectivity. We feel that to insist the social sciences move in the direction of inclusiveness (in terms of the recruitment of personnel, an openness to multiple cultural experiences, the scope of legitimate matters of study) is to further the possibility of more objective knowledge. We feel that to emphasize the historicity of all social phenomena is to diminish the tendency to make premature, and ultimately naive, abstractions from reality. We feel that persistently to question the subjective elements in our theoretical models is to increase the likelihood that these models will be relevant and useful. We feel that attention to the three issues we have previously discussed – a better appreciation of the validity of the ontological distinction between humans and nature, a broader definition of the boundaries within which social action occurs, and a proper balance of the antinomy of universalism and particularism – will all assist considerably our attempts to develop the kind of more valid knowledge that we seek to have.

In short, the fact that knowledge is socially constructed also means that more valid knowledge is socially possible. The recognition of the social bases of knowledge is not at all in contradiction to the concept of objectivity. On the contrary, we argue that the restructuring of the social sciences of which we have been speaking can amplify this possibility by taking into account the criticisms of past practice that have been made and by building structures that are more truly pluralist and universal.

# IV.  Conclusion: Restructuring the Social Sciences

We have tried in this report to address three things. The first is to show how social science was historically constructed as a form of knowledge and why it was divided into a specific set of relatively standard disciplines in a process that went on between the late eighteenth century and 1945. The second is to reveal the ways in which world developments in the period since 1945 raised questions about this intellectual division of labor and therefore reopened the issues of organizational structuring that had been put into place in the previous period. The third is to elucidate a series of basic intellectual questions about which there has been much recent debate and to suggest a stance that we think optimal in order to move forward. We now turn to discussing in what ways the social sciences might be intelligently restructured in the light of this history and the recent debates.

We should say at the outset we have no simple, clearcut formulas, but primarily present a set of tentative proposals that seem to us to move in the right direction. There is unclarity today in the classification of the social sciences, the result of various blurrings whose historical roots we have tried to explain. To be sure, adjustments can always be made, and indeed are constantly being made, that can ameliorate some of the irrationalities. We certainly do not advocate abolishing the idea of divisions of labor within social science, and this may continue to take the form of disciplines. Disciplines serve a function, the function of disciplining minds and channeling scholarly energy. But there has to be some level of consensus about the validity of the dividing lines, if they are to work. We have tried to indicate the ways that the historical trajectory of the institutionalization of the social sciences led to some major exclusions of reality. Discussion about these exclusions has meant that the level of consensus concerning the traditional disciplines has diminished.

The classification of the social sciences was constructed around two antinomies which no longer command the wide support they once enjoyed: the antinomy between past and present, and the antinomy between idiographic and nomothetic disciplines. A third antinomy, that between the civilized and the barbaric world, has few public defenders anymore, but in practice still inhabits the mentalities of many scholars.

In addition to the intellectual debates surrounding the logic of the present disciplinary divisions, there is the problem of resources. The principal administrative mode of dealing with protests about the present divisions has been the multiplication of interdisciplinary programs of training and research, a process that is continuing unabated, as additional claims are still constantly being made. But such multiplication requires personnel and money. However, the reality of the world of knowledge of the 1990's, especially as compared to that of earlier decades, is the constraint on resources imposed by fiscal crises in almost every state. While social scientists, because of the internal pressures generated by their intellectual dilemmas, are seeking to expand the number and variety of pedagogical and research structures, administrators are looking for ways to economize and therefore to consolidate. We are not suggesting that there has been too much multidisciplinarity. Far from it. Rather, we are pointing out that organizationally this has gone less in the direction of unifying activities than in that of multiplying the number of university names and programs.

It is only a matter of time for the two contrary pressures to collide, and collide severely. We may hope that working social scientists will take a hard look at their present structures and try to bring their revised intellectual perceptions of a useful division of labor into line with the organizational framework they necessarily construct. If working social scientists do not do this, it will no doubt be done for them by administrators of the institutions of knowledge. To be sure, no one is, or is likely to be, in a position to decree wholesale reorganization, nor would it necessarily be a good thing if someone were. Nonetheless, the alternative to wholesale, sudden, and dramatic reorganization is not muddling through, expecting that somehow things will improve and work themselves out. This is because confusion, overlap, and resource shortage are all increasing simultaneously, and together they can add up to a major blockage in the furtherance of knowledge.

Let us remember a further reality of the present situation. While we have been describing a general pattern in the social sciences today, the detailed classifications vary country by country, often institution by institution. Furthermore, the degree of internal cohesiveness and flexibility of the disciplines varies today, both between disciplines and among the forms a discipline assumes around the world. The pressure for change therefore is not uniform. In addition, the pressure for change varies according to the theoretical perspectives of various social scientists, and according to the degree to which particular groups of social scientists are more or less directly involved in public service activities and concerns. Finally, different communities of social scientists find themselves in different political situations—national political situations, university political situations—and these differences affect their interests and therefore the degree to which they will favor or strongly oppose administrative reorganization.

No doubt, we could simply plead for more flexibility. This is the course that we have in fact been following for three or four decades now. There has been a certain amount of success in this regard, but the alleviation of the problem has not kept pace with its intensification. The reason is simple. The sense of safety in the disciplines tends more often than not to win out in the small group arenas that university departments constitute, and in which much of the real power of day-to-day decision making is located. Foundations may give grants to imaginative groups of scholars, but departments decide on promotions or course curricula. Good motivations pronounced by individuals are not always very efficacious in constraining organizational pressures.

What seems to be called for is less an attempt to transform organizational frontiers than to amplify the organization of intellectual activity without attention to current disciplinary boundaries. To be historical is after all not the exclusive purview of persons called historians. It is an obligation of all social scientists. To be sociological is not the exclusive purview of persons called sociologists. It is an obligation of all social scientists. Economic issues are not the exclusive purview of economists. Economic questions are central to any and all social scientific analyses. Nor is it absolutely sure that professional historians necessarily know more about historical explanations, sociologists more about social issues, economists more about economic fluctuations than other working social scientists. In short, we do not believe that there are monopolies of wisdom, nor zones of knowledge reserved to persons with particular university degrees.

There are emerging, to be sure, particular groupings of social scientists (and indeed non-social scientists) around specified interests or thematic areas, from population to health to language, and so forth. There are emerging groupings around the level of analysis (concentration on individual social action; concentration on large-scale, long-term social processes). Whether or not the thematic distinctions or the "micro/macro" distinction are ideal ways to organize the division of labor in social science knowledge today, they may be at least as plausible as distinguishing between the economic and the political, for example.

Where do opportunities for creative experimentation lie? There must be many which the reader can identify. We can point to some that are found at quite different loci on the academic spectrum. At one extreme lies the United States, with the largest density of university structures in the world, and also a very strong internal political pressure both for and against restructuring the social sciences. At the other extreme lies Africa, where universities are of relatively recent construction and the traditional disciplines are not very strongly institutionalized. There the extreme paucity of public resources has created a situation in which the social science community has been forced to innovate. No doubt, there are particularities elsewhere in the world, which will permit equally interesting experimentation. One such arena is perhaps the post-Communist countries, where much academic reorganization is occurring. And no doubt, as Western Europe builds its community structures, there will be openings for creative experimentation in the university system.

In the United States, university structures are multiple, diverse, and decentralized. The issues raised by the call for multiculturalism, as well as the work in science studies, have already become the subject of public political debate. Issues raised by some of the new developments in science may possibly be caught in the political whirl by contagion. This provides an additional motive for working social scientists to take the issues in hand and to try thereby to keep passing (and passionate) political considerations from intruding too deeply in a process that is far too consequential to be decided on electoral motivations. The United States has had a long history of structural experimentation in the university systems – the invention of graduate schools in the late nineteenth century, a modification of the German seminar system; the invention of the system of free electives by

students, also in the late nineteenth century; the invention of
social science research councils after the First World War; the
invention of "core course" requirements after the First World
War; the invention of area studies after the Second World War;
the invention of women's studies and "ethnic" programs of multiple kinds in the 1970's. We are not taking a position for or
against any of these inventions, but use them to illustrate the
fact that there has been room in the U.S. university system to ex-
periment. Perhaps the U.S. social science community can once
again come up with imaginative solutions to the very real organizational problems we have been describing.

   In the post-Communist countries, we are faced with a situation in which many erstwhile structures have been disbanded
and certain university categories discarded. The financial pressures have been such that many scholars have moved outside the
university structures to continue their work. As a consequence,
here too there seems much room for experimentation. There is,
of course, the risk that scholars will seek to adopt wholesale the
existing structures of Western universities on the grounds that
these represent a future that is different from their own immediate past, without recognizing the real difficulties in which the
Western university systems are finding themselves. Nonetheless, there are some signs of experimentation. For example, in
erstwhile East Germany, at Humboldt University in Berlin, the
history department has become the first one in Germany, perhaps in Europe, to create a subdepartment of European ethnol-
ogy, attempting thereby to give so-called historical anthropology a *droit de cité* inside of history. Historical anthropology has
also become a formal category within the Ecole des Hautes

Etudes en Sciences Sociales in Paris, there not within history, but side by side as coequal with both history and social anthropology. At the same time, in a number of universities in various parts of the world, physical anthropology has come to be incorporated into human biology.

The European Community has placed considerable importance on strengthening links among its various universities, through exchange programs and the encouragement of new pan-European research projects. The universities are seeking to face creatively the question of the multiplicity of languages in scholarly use, and we may hope that the solutions they find may restore the linguistic richness of social scientific activity and offer some answers to one of the issues raised under the relationship of universalism and particularism. Insofar as there may be new universities created with a specifically European vocation (one example may be the Europa-Universität Viadrina in Frankfurt an Oder), there exists the opportunity to restructure the social sciences without having the problem of transforming existing organizational structures.

In Africa, a process of experimentation has already begun. The current situation in Africa, which in many ways looks dismal, has provided a foundation for alternative forms of scholarship which do not necessarily reflect the disciplinary approaches adopted in other regions of the world. Much of the research about socioeconomic evolution has required that research methods not be fixed but rather open to accommodate new knowledge and has encouraged cutting across the divide between the social and natural sciences. Experimentation has also occurred in other parts of the non-Western world. The same dilemma of

limited resources and lack of deep institutionalization of the social science disciplines led to the creation in the past thirty years
of the very successful FLACSO (Facultad Latinoamericana de
Ciencias Sociales) research and training structures throughout
Latin America, which have operated as para-university institutions not beholden to traditional categories of knowledge.

The emergence of independent research institutions in Africa
and Latin America, although they are still limited in number,
has created an alternative avenue for undertaking research. One
of the interesting features of some of these institutions is that
they seek to join together expertise from the social and the natural sciences, showing little regard for disciplinary boundaries.
They have also become major sources of policy ideas for government officials. This is now also occurring in the post-Communist countries. It has, of course, also occurred in Western countries. The Science Policy Research Unit at Sussex University has
a curriculum that is divided half and half between the social and
natural sciences.

While it is not yet possible to be sure that the emerging social
science research in these new frameworks will result in coherent
alternative groupings of knowledge, it is safe to say that in some
parts of the world the old paradigms and the institutions that
were set up to safeguard, nurture, and protect them never really
worked or have broken down. Such regions did not fully enter
the old intellectual cul-de-sacs and therefore they are now relatively more open spaces in which intellectual and institutional
innovations are emerging. This self-organizing trend, emerging
from relatively chaotic situations, may serve to encourage us to
support other such self-organizing trends outside the accepted
paths of the world university system.

We are not at a moment when the existing disciplinary structure has broken down. We are at a point when it has been questioned and when competing structures are trying to come into existence. We think the most urgent task is that there be comprehensive discussion of the underlying issues. This is the primary function of this report, to encourage such discussion and to elaborate the interconnected issues that have arisen. In addition, we think there are at least four kinds of structural developments which administrators of structures of social science knowledge (university administrators, social science research councils, ministries of education and/or research, educational foundations, UNESCO, international social science organizations, etc.) could and should encourage as useful paths towards intellectual clarification and eventual fuller restructuring of the social sciences:

1. *The expansion of institutions, within or allied to the universities, which would bring together scholars for a year's work in common around specific urgent themes.* They already exist, of course, but in far too limited a number. One possible model is the ZiF (Zentrum für interdisziplinäre Forschung) at Bielefeld University in Germany, which has done this since the 1970's. Recent topics for the year have included body and soul, sociological and biological models of change, utopias. The crucial thing is that such year-long research groups should be carefully prepared in advance and should recruit their membership widely (in terms of disciplines, geography, cultural and linguistic zones, and gender), while still emphasizing enough coherence with previous views so that the interchange can be fruitful.

2. *The establishment of integrated research programs within university structures that cut across traditional lines, have*

*specific intellectual objectives, and have funds for a limited period of time (say about five years).* This is different from traditional research centers, which have unlimited lives and are expected to be fund-raising structures. The ad hoc quality of such programs, which would, however, last five years, would be a mechanism of constant experimentation, which, once initially funded, would free the participants from this concern. In the multitude of requests for new programs, instead of immediately starting new teaching programs, perhaps what is needed is that the proponents be allowed to demonstrate the utility and validity of their approaches by this kind of research program.

3. *The compulsory joint appointment of professors.* Today the norm is that professors are affiliated with one department, usually one in which they themselves have an advanced degree. Occasionally, and more or less as a special concession, some professors have a "joint appointment" with a second department. Quite often this is a mere courtesy, and the professor is not encouraged to participate too actively in the life of the "second" or "secondary" department. We would like to turn this around entirely. We would envisage a university structure in which everyone was appointed to two departments, the one in which he/she had his degree and a second one in which he/she had shown interest or done relevant work. This would, of course, result in an incredible array of different combinations. Furthermore, in order to make sure that no department erected barriers, we would require that each department have at least 25 percent of its members who did *not* have a degree in that discipline. If the professors then had *full* rights in both departments, the intellectual debate within each department, the curricula offered, the points

of view that were considered plausible or legitimate would all change as a result of this simple administrative device.

4. *Joint work for graduate students.* The situation is the same for graduate students as it is for professors. They normally work within one department, and are often actively discouraged from doing any work at all in a second department. Only in a few departments in a few universities are students allowed to wander outside. We would turn this around too. Why not make it mandatory for students seeking a doctorate in a given discipline to take a certain number of courses, or do a certain amount of research, that is defined as being within the purview of a second department? This too would result in an incredible variety of combinations. Administered in a liberal but serious fashion, it would transform the present and the future.

While the first two recommendations we make would require financial commitments on someone's part, they should not be too onerous as a percentage of total expenditures on the social sciences. The third and the fourth recommendations would be virtually without any budgetary impact whatsoever. We do not intend these recommendations to be limiting. We intend them to encourage moves in the correct direction. There are no doubt other devices that can also move in this direction, and we encourage others to propose them. What is most important, we repeat, is that the underlying issues be debated – clearly, openly, intelligently, and urgently.

*Library of Congress*
*Cataloging-in-Publication Data*

Gulbenkian Commission on the Restructuring of the Social Sciences.
Open the social sciences : report of the Gulbenkian Commission on
the Restructuring of the Social Sciences.
    p.    cm. – (Mestizo spaces = Espaces métisses)
    Includes bibliographical references.
    ISBN 0-8047-2726-0 (cloth : alk. paper). – ISBN 0-8047-2727-9
(pbk. : alk. paper)
    1. Social sciences.  I. Title.  II. Series: Mestizo spaces.
H61.G864   1996
300–dc20
95-45759  CIP

⊗ This book is printed on acid-free, recycled paper.

Original printing 1996
Last figure below indicates year of this printing:
05 04 03 02 01 00 99 98 97 96

nomothetic.

- law making / legislature
concerned with making general
scientific laws.